COMMUNICATION CAMPAIGNS ABOUT DRUGS:

Government, Media, and the Public

COMMUNICATION TEXTBOOK SERIES

Jennings Bryant – Editor

Journalism
Maxwell McCombs – Advisor

BERNER • Writing Literary
Features

FENSCH • The Sports Writing
Handbook

TITCHENER • Reviewing
the Arts

FENSCH • Writing Solutions
Beginnings, Middles,
and Endings

SHOEMAKER • Communication
Campaigns about Drugs:
Government, Media,
and the Public

COMMUNICATION CAMPAIGNS ABOUT DRUGS:

Government, Media, and the Public

Edited by
Pamela J. Shoemaker
University of Texas at Austin

LEA *LAWRENCE ERLBAUM ASSOCIATES, PUBLISHERS*
1989   *Hillsdale, New Jersey*   *Hove and London*

Lawrence Erlbaum Associates, Inc., Publishers
365 Broadway
Hillsdale, New Jersey 07642

Library of Congress Cataloging-in-Publication Data

Communication campaigns about drugs: government, media, and the
public / edited by Pamela J. Shoemaker.
    p.   cm.
  Includes indexes.
  ISBN 0-8058-0230-4
    1. Drugs and mass media—United States—Congresses.   2. Drug
abuse—United States—Prevention—Congresses.   3. Narcotics, Control
of—United States—Congresses.   I. Shoemaker, Pamela J.
  HV5825.C619   1989   88-22760
  362.2′93—dc19   CIP

Printed in the United States of America
10 9 8 7 6 5 4 3 2 1

Contents

6

7

8

9

10

DEALING WITH ILLICIT DRUGS: THE POWER – AND LIMITS –
OF MASS MEDIA AGENDA SETTING
Donald L. Shaw and Maxwell E. McCombs   113

Preface

Work on what eventually became this book began in late 1986, when Phil Meyer, program chair for the 1987 American Association for Public Opinion Research annual conference, asked me to coordinate a panel on whether the previous months' heavy dose of drug coverage in the mass media had affected public opinion. As I recall, Max McCombs and Don Shaw had already turned down the project; as an assistant professor, I found it difficult to turn down anything.

After numerous phone calls, I was able to offer Phil a panel that covered the topic from "soup to nuts," from the federal government's antidrug public information campaign, to media coverage of drugs, to public concern with drugs, to measures of drug use. Avraham Forman and Susan Lachter, of the National Institute on Drug Abuse, agreed to prepare a paper on their "Just Say No" and "Cocaine, The Big Lie" campaigns. John Merriam, Conference on Issues and Media, proved willing to write an overview of how national media coverage of drugs had changed over time. My colleagues at the University of Texas at Austin—Steve Reese, Lucig Danielian, Wayne Wanta, and Dawn Leggett—agreed to investigate both influences on media content and how the media might affect public opinion. Lloyd Johnston, University of Michigan, was finally persuaded to contribute a paper on how high school seniors' drug use had changed. Don Shaw, University of North Carolina, agreed to participate in the panel as a respondent to the five papers.

I am grateful to these individuals for their willingness not only to contribute to the AAPOR panel, but also for their efforts in revising and expanding on their AAPOR papers for publication in the book in a timely fashion. Lachter and Forman wrote a second chapter that provided background information on the drug problem and on the National Institute on Drug Abuse's reactions to it. Reese and Danielian did additional analyses on intermedia agenda setting and wrote a second chapter. Dorothy Davidson Nesbit agreed to contribute and rework her AAPOR paper on attitudes toward drug testing. Shaw and McCombs agreed to write a summary chapter that established the relationship of the research to the agenda-setting literature.

I am also grateful to Phil Meyer for suggesting that I begin work on this topic and to Max McCombs for his continual support and suggestions during the preparation of this book.

Pamela J. Shoemaker

1

Introduction

Pamela J. Shoemaker
University of Texas

When the U.S. government wants to influence its citizens, it does so through the mass media. This book is about one such campaign and its effects. The government's "war on drugs" in the mid-1980s was designed to reduce demand for illegal drugs by educating the public about the dangers of drugs and hence changing its attitudes toward drugs. The war was waged on the battleground of the nation's newspapers, television networks, and news magazines, with the media not only voluntarily running government public service announcements for free, but also dramatically increasing their news coverage of illegal drugs during 1986. Public concern with illegal drugs rose during the period.

Although the war on drugs culminated during the Reagan administration, Susan Lachter and Avraham Forman point out in chapter 2 that its roots are in the turbulent 1960s. The widespread use of marijuana by young adults and experimentation with hallucinogenic drugs such as LSD on college campuses led to efforts in 1972 by the federal government to stop the drug trade. In 1974 the National Institute on Drug Abuse (NIDA) was created and given the continuing responsibility for research on illegal drugs and for developing treatment and prevention programs.

NIDA's research showed that Americans' use of illegal drugs steadily increased throughout the 1970s and that public awareness of the dangers of drug use was low. Based on these data, NIDA was given the go ahead in 1982 to prepare a major educational campaign aimed at teenagers and their parents. One measure of this campaign's success is the fact that these "Just Say No" public service announcements were still running at the time this book went to press.

In 1984 NIDA's attention focused on cocaine use, which had increasingly been involved in emergency room episodes and drug-related deaths during the early 1980s. The first public service announcement in the "Cocaine, The Big Lie" campaign went on the air in April 1986.

Although media coverage of illegal drugs steadily increased during the early 1980s, the biggest increase in media emphasis on drugs occurred during the summer and early fall of 1986. The media experienced what Reese and Danielian call (in chapter 5) a "feeding frenzy," converging on the drug story out of proportion, some suggested, to the size of the problem. As Peter Kerr (1986) pointed out in his *New York Times* article, the sudden increase in media attention to drugs during the summer of 1986 could not be explained as merely reflecting the real world. Although drug use had steadily increased during the 1970s, active drug use among high school seniors and young adults (see chapter 9) actually declined between 1981 and 1986. Most of the decline was in usage of marijuana; cocaine use remained steady.

If the sudden increase in media coverage during 1986 could not be explained by an increase in drug use, then what did cause it? What effect has media coverage of drugs had on public concern with drugs? In other words, who set the media agenda and what impact did the media agenda have on the public agenda?

The term *agenda setting* was introduced by McCombs and Shaw to describe a process through which the mass media may influence how much importance the public places on various issues: The more the media emphasize an issue, the more importance the public places on it. Most early agenda-setting studies looked at the relationship between the media agenda and the public agenda, although more recently scholars have studied the formation of both the media agenda and the policy agenda.

This book deals with all three agendas. In chapters 2 and 3, Susan Lachter and Avraham Forman describe how the federal government's policy agenda was set during the 1960s and 1970s by both anecdotal and empirical evidence about Americans' use of illegal drugs. The National Institute on Drug Abuse's reaction was to begin public education programs designed to ultimately reduce the demand for illegal drugs, while in the short run providing information about the dangers of drugs and treatment programs for addicted individuals.

These public education programs—"Just Say No" and "Cocaine, The Big Lie"—shaped both the media and public agendas. Not only did NIDA's public service announcements directly activate public concern with drugs, but they also helped focus the mass media's attention on drugs. In chapter 4, John Merriam charts fluctuations in national media coverage of drugs over time with drug-related events. Although media coverage of drugs did increase during the "Just Say No" campaign in 1985, the deaths of two Drug Enforcement Administration agents in Mexico may have accentuated effects of the campaign. The big media push, of course, came in the summer of 1986, not long after NIDA ran its first "Cocaine, The Big Lie" public service announcement, and around the time that Maryland basketball player Len Bias died from a cocaine overdose. By the time that the Reagan White House announced its "war on drugs" in late summer 1986, media coverage was starting to wane.

In addition to charting fluctuations in drug coverage, Merriam compared the "life" of the drug issue with other issues and discusses how competition from other issues may have affected where the drug issue fell on the media agenda. He also points out how the drug story changed from primarily being oriented toward drug crimes in 1983 to drug abuse in 1986.

In chapters 5 and 6, Stephen Reese and Lucig Danielian investigate the extent to which the overall national media agenda may be influenced from within – by the "convergence" of individual media around the drug story. Defining convergence as similarities of timing, emphasis, and source selection in an issue's coverage among the mass media, Reese and Danielian suggest that it may be most likely to occur when the story is not purely event driven, as was the case with the drug issue.

Looking at media coverage of cocaine during 1985 and 1986, Reese and Danielian conclude that the major media did cover cocaine in a similar way at roughly the same time, and the evidence also suggests that the print media may set the agendas for the television networks and news magazines. The result is that, although there were many different media carrying the drug story, the diversity of that information was low. The media converged on the drug issue, influencing each other in both the amount and type of coverage given to drugs.

Chapter 7 addresses the linkage between media coverage of drugs and public opinion. Using data from 43 Gallup polls on the "most important problem facing America today," Pamela Shoemaker, Wayne Wanta, and Dawn Leggett correlate public concern about drugs with 15 years of drug coverage in three newspapers, three television networks, and three news magazines. Newspaper coverage (especially of *The New York Times* and *The Los Angeles Times*) turns out to be the best predictor of public opinion.

When Shoemaker, Wanta, and Leggett compare drug coverage in each of the 6 months preceding each Gallup poll with the poll data, they find that public opinion is best predicted by media coverage in the first and fourth months preceding each poll. This suggests that the biggest effects on the public agenda may occur when media coverage recurs on a 3- or 4-month cycle.

Dorothy Davidson Nesbit takes a different look at public opinion in chapter 8. During the 1986 period of media hype, Nesbit studied public attitudes toward drug testing on the job. She demonstrates that public support for drug testing is soft, being affected by the information that the individual holds about the accuracy of drug testing. When told that drug testing may be inaccurate or that urine samples must be given under observation, many supporters of testing withdrew their support. Opposition to testing, on the other hand, is firm unless the individual's job is at stake.

In chapter 9, Lloyd Johnston draws on his unusual position as a participant–observer during the time of intense media drug coverage in 1986. As a result of his longitudinal study of high school seniors' drug use since 1975, Johnston estimates that he participated in between 200 and 300 press interviews about drug use. His data show that overall drug use *declined* between 1981 and 1986–during the same period in which NIDA undertook its public information campaign and in which mass media coverage of drugs increased.

When Johnston studied cocaine use separately from that of other drugs, however, he found that its use did not decline during the 1980s but rather remained steady, even in the face of the NIDA "Cocaine, The Big Lie" campaign. In addition, cocaine's involvement in drug-related deaths and hospital emergency room visits increased dramatically during the 1980s, giving the media and the public many examples of cocaine's harmfulness.

Was the 1986 media coverage of drugs "live or Memorex?" Johnston asks. In the final analysis, Johnston defends the media's attention to drugs as reflecting not the overall usage of drugs by the American public, but the use of cocaine, an especially addictive and harmful drug that was increasingly picking up younger users. The drug crisis of 1986 was a different one than that of 1979 or 1980, Johnston writes, but the seriousness of cocaine justified media attention to it.

Although the media may have been educated throughout 1985 and 1986 about the dangers of cocaine by the National Institute on Drug Abuse's information campaign, and to that extent NIDA may have influenced the media agenda, the media were also reacting to a real problem–more use of cocaine among the young in increasingly dangerous forms. If the public became more concerned about drug use in the 1980s, the public issue agenda may have been influenced by NIDA's "Just Say No" and "Cocaine, The Big Lie" campaigns by other media coverage of drugs, but it may also have been influenced by increasing personal experience with drugs in the schools and workplace. As Donald Shaw and Maxwell McCombs point out in chapter 10, ascribing hypodermic-like powers to NIDA or the mass media would be too simple. News is created in reaction to events in the "real" world, but journalists' assessments of an issue's newsworthiness are also affected by their personal opinions experiences, by public relations efforts of the government and special interest groups, by the audience, by what other media are doing, by deadlines, and by a plethora of other factors.

Did the National Institute on Drug Abuse's public information campaigns affect the media and public agendas? Almost certainly. But the power of such campaigns to affect the media agenda is limited. Not only is the presence of a communication campaign unsupported by an observable and important problem unlikely to receive substantial media coverage or significant public attention, but also campaign materials must compete with other potential media content. The result is that, even with sufficient justification, media coverage may not be forthcoming, or the public's behaviors may prove difficult to change.

Did the media's coverage of illegal drugs affect the public's concern with drugs? Probably. But, although the media can throw spotlights on problems and, perhaps, help move them higher on the public agenda, they cannot by themselves solve social problems. A solution to America's drug problem will involve a complex relationship among the parties involved. No one participant—neither the federal government, nor the media, nor the public—can solve the problem alone.

REFERENCE

Kerr, P. (1986, November 17). Anatomy of an issue: Drugs, the evidence, the reaction. *New York Times,* pp. 1, 12.

2

Drug Abuse in the United States

Susan B. Lachter
Avraham Forman
National Institute on Drug Abuse

Although illicit drug use had long been a problem in the United States, the public did not begin to recognize how drug abuse threatened all parts of society until the late 1960s. From college campuses to the city streets, people experimented with drugs that changed their thoughts, their feelings, and the way they viewed the world. It was the "psychedelic" era.

The problems of widespread drug abuse soon became apparent. Hallucinogenic drugs such as LSD were being used by thousands of college students, who often experienced frightening psychological effects. Marijuana came into vogue as a perceived harmless, "recreational" drug, whose use soon became a symbol of rebelliousness for certain segments of college youth and young adults. And heroin use in America's turbulent cities would soon lead to a growing public awareness that something had to be done to deal with the drug problem.

By 1972, the federal government recognized that strong measures needed to be taken to stop trafficking in illicit drugs and to provide treatment for those who were addicted. Those efforts, initiated by the White House Special Action Office for Drug Abuse Prevention, led to the development of a nationwide drug abuse treatment system, the initiation of research into the nature and extent of the drug problem, and drug abuse prevention programs designed to help youth. In 1974, the National Institute on Drug Abuse (NIDA) was established to continue these activities.

Today NIDA, which is a part of the U.S. Department of Health and Human Services, is the primary federal agency responsible for reducing the demand for illicit drugs. The Institute sponsors and conducts research on the causes and consequences of drug abuse and on the development of effective treatment and prevention approaches. NIDA's continuing responsibility for monitoring the nature and extent of the drug problem provides direction for public and private program development and planning.

NATIONAL HOUSEHOLD SURVEY ON DRUG USE

NIDA sponsors three major epidemiological programs to collect information on the incidence and prevalence of drug abuse and its health consequences. The first, the National Household Survey on Drug Use, monitors the drug-use patterns of the general public over the age of 12 (National Institute on Drug Abuse, 1987b). This survey has been conducted every 2 to 3 years since 1972. Approximately 8,000 people are interviewed each time, and the sample's demographic breakdown is representative of the national population.

NIDA projects the survey results against the U.S. census in order to estimate illicit drug use among Americans 12 years old or older (National Institute on Drug Abuse, 1987c). According to the 1985 survey, 70.4 million Americans (representing 37% of those who are at least 12 years old) have used marijuana, cocaine, or other illicit drugs at least once during their lifetimes. Nearly 37 million (19%) used illicit drugs within the year prior to being surveyed (termed *annual use*), and 23 million (12%) used illicit drugs at least once within the month immediately prior to the survey (termed *current use*). With one in eight Americans estimated to be current users of illicit drugs in 1985, it is apparent that drug use is still a significant phenomenon in society.

The Household Survey shows that there was a dramatic increase between 1972 and 1979 in both current and annual marijuana use among all age groups, but that marijuana use continually declined from 1979 to 1985. Cocaine use showed a different trend. Although both current and annual cocaine use peaked in 1979 for young adults (ages 18 to 25), cocaine use among teenagers (12 to 17) and older adults (26 and older) continued to increase.

Specifically, current use of marijuana among young adults, the group with the highest drug use, increased from 27.8% in 1972 to a high of 35.5% in 1979 but then declined to 21.9% by 1985. Among teenagers, current marijuana use increased from 7% in 1972 to 16.7% in 1979 and then declined to 12.3% by 1985.

Measurement of cocaine use began in 1974, when 3.1% of young adults reported current usage. This increased to 9.3% in 1979 but declined to 7.7% by 1985. Although cocaine use is primarily limited to those 18 years old and older, there was a steady increase in usage among teenagers between 1974 (.6% reporting current use) and 1985 (1.8%).

NATIONAL HIGH SCHOOL SENIOR SURVEY

The trends illustrating that 1979 was a year of very high drug use have been confirmed by similar data from the second of NIDA's three major epidemiological programs–the Monitoring the Future Survey of high school seniors, also known as the National High School Senior Survey (Johnston, O'Malley, & Bachman, 1987). This survey of approximately 17,000 high school seniors has been conducted annually since 1975. Surveying drug use by high school seniors is a conservative, but reliable approach to monitoring trends among the adolescent population. Although the survey does not include data from youngsters who have dropped out of the school system, the number of dropouts is small relative to the nationwide population of high school seniors and does not significantly affect the overall percentages of drug use.

The High School Senior Survey parallels the results of the Household Survey population for teenagers. The highest marijuana-using years among high school seniors were 1978 and 1979, but cocaine use remained high through 1986.

Current marijuana use among high school seniors rose from 27.1% in 1975 to a high of 37.1% in 1978 but declined to 23.4% by 1986. Current use of cocaine among seniors rose from 1.9% in 1975 to 5.7% in 1979 and was 6.2% in 1986. The highest usage level came in 1985, when 6.7% of surveyed seniors reported using cocaine.

In addition to monitoring drug use among high school seniors, this survey also reports seniors' attitudes and beliefs about drug use, such as how harmful they think drugs are, how much they personally disapprove of drug use, and their attitudes on the legality of using various drugs in different circumstances.

NIDA uses information about student attitudes when designing public education programs, because the reported attitudes often provide clues about the kinds of messages needed to encourage attitude or behavior change. The seniors' attitudes also provide information about the need for public education in particular areas. For example, from 1975 through 1978 there was a decline in the percentage of high school seniors who saw regular marijuana use as being harmful (43.3% to 34.9%). When NIDA saw that 8% fewer high school seniors rated marijuana as harmful in 1978 than in 1975, the agency released information about marijuana's harmful effects to counteract teenagers' lack of awareness. Subsequent information distributed by the private sector also contributed to a new appreciation for marijuana's adverse consequences, especially on young people.

The downward trend in ratings of marijuana's harmfulness reversed in 1979, when 42% of high school seniors saw a "great risk" in regular marijuana use. By 1986 this figure rose to 71.3%. Accompanying this trend in beliefs about marijuana's harmfulness was a significant decrease in all measures of marijuana use. Daily use showed the biggest decline, dropping from nearly 11% in 1978 to 4% in 1986.

Similar changes in attitudes occurred concerning the perceived harmfulness of regular use of cocaine. Although in 1975 cocaine was seen as harmful by 73% of seniors, by 1978 this figure had dropped to 68%. By 1980, 70% of seniors rated cocaine as harmful, and this increased to 82% in 1986.

Perceptions of the risk involved in experimenting with cocaine did not change much during these periods; 34% of seniors rated cocaine experimentation as risky in 1986, compared with 31% in 1980. Such low levels of concern about cocaine experimentation have led to concern about new users among those who are young, vulnerable, and therefore at extreme risk for cocaine's dependence-producing effects. There is hope that the widespread media reports about cocaine's contributing to basketball player Len Bias' death and the extensive broadcast of NIDA's "Cocaine, The Big Lie" campaign will lead to increased awareness of the dangers of experimenting with the drug.

DRUG ABUSE WARNING NETWORK

NIDA's third source of epidemiologic data is the Drug Abuse Warning Network, which monitors reports on people who come to hospital emergency rooms for drug abuse-related health problems and reviews medical examiners' reports on individuals who die from drug abuse-related causes (National Institute on Drug Abuse, 1978a). In 1986 the Drug Abuse Warning Network received reports from 744 hospital emergency rooms and from 75 medical examiners in 27 metropolitan areas around the country. Reported medical problems included overdose and toxic reactions to drugs, as well as less obvious consequences of drug use such as driving and workplace accidents and long-term damage to the heart, lungs, and other organs.

In 1986 the most frequently reported drugs in these emergency room episodes were cocaine (24,847 mentions), alcohol in combination with other drugs (21,801), heroin/morphine (15,832), diazepam (7,653), PCP and PCP combinations (6,421), and marijuana (6,046). This was the first year that emergency room episodes involving cocaine use exceeded those involving alcohol in combination with other drugs.

Cocaine was used in combination with other drugs in approximately half of the emergency room episodes. Cocaine was smoked or injected in 51% of the cases and sniffed in 23%. It is clear that smoking or injecting cocaine results in more severe health consequences than does sniffing it.

In medical examiners' reports, the most frequently mentioned drug was heroin or morphine (1,549 mentions). Alcohol in combination with other drugs was mentioned in 1,463 of the reported deaths, and cocaine was involved in 1,092 of the deaths. Seventy percent of the deaths reported by medical examiners were directly caused by drugs; drug abuse was related to, but did not directly cause, the remaining deaths.

CONCLUSIONS

After reviewing the national trends in attitudes and behaviors of the late 1970s and early 1980s, it became clear to NIDA that public awareness of the dangers of drug abuse was very low. The Institute was concerned that a broad spectrum of the public was involved in drug use, particularly teenagers, and that parents and other adults had to take action to prevent the onset of drug use among young children. In 1982, NIDA used all of its drug use and attitude data to design the "Just Say No" information campaign that was aimed primarily at junior high school students and their parents. Its goal was to present a drug-free life as the healthy norm for teenagers; drug use would no longer be a rite of passage for America's youth.

"Just Say No" provided a slogan and a concept for national public and private sector activities in drug abuse prevention. Changing public attitudes about drug use are helping to change the school and work environment across America. For healthy youngsters and responsible adults, drug use cannot be tolerated. The historical data show that the absence of public education programs can often lead to a return to a tolerance of drug use as it did in the late 1970s. People need to be reminded about the social and health consequences of drug abuse as a key to a healthy society.

REFERENCES

Johnston, L.D., O'Malley, P.M., & Bachman, J.G. (1987). *National trends in drug use and related factors among American high school students and young adults. 1975–1986*. Washington, DC: U.S. Government Printing Office.

National Institute on Drug Abuse. (1987a). *Drug Abuse Warning Network (DAWN). Annual report 1986*. Washington, DC: U.S. Government Printing Office.

National Institute on Drug Abuse. (1987b). *Highlights from the National Survey on Drug Abuse.* Rockville, MD: National Institute on Drug Abuse.

National Institute on Drug Abuse (1987c). *Population projections, based on the National Survey on Drug Abuse.* Washington, DC: U.S. Government Printing Office.

3

The National Institute on Drug Abuse Cocaine Prevention Campaign

Avraham Forman
Susan B. Lachter
National Institute on Drug Abuse

To counter increasing cocaine use among older teenagers and young adults, the National Institute on Drug Abuse (NIDA) developed a multimedia Cocaine Abuse Prevention Campaign, called "Cocaine, The Big Lie." The first of two phases was launched in April 1986. This public service campaign, developed by Needham Harper Worldwide, under the auspices of the Advertising Council, Inc., targeted 18- to 35-year-olds with messages about the addictive qualities of cocaine, its potential for producing severe health consequences, and the need to seek treatment.

Phase 1 of the campaign included radio and television public service announcements and print advertisements that featured real people from all walks of life who have been addicted to cocaine. They described the seductive and addictive qualities of the drug and the devastating effect it had on their own health, career, and relationships. Sports celebrities and the First Lady also appealed to users to get help and to nonusers to avoid trying cocaine. A second phase, which began Spring 1988, targeted messages to high school and college students as well as to families and friends of users.

The purpose of this chapter is to describe NIDA's experience in developing this media campaign, which was based on the results of scientific research and which has been used as a tool to affect the public's perception of and behavior toward drug abuse.

THE PROBLEM

From 1982 reports of NIDA's National Household Survey, it was estimated that between 20 and 24 million Americans had tried cocaine at least once in their lives. Between 11 and 13 million Americans had used cocaine during the previous year, and between 3 and 5 million used cocaine during the past month. Young adults (ages 18 to 25) showed the highest percentage of lifetime cocaine use: 28% had tried the drug at least once during their lives. The survey also showed that the cocaine use was high among all income and class groups, despite the public's perception that only the rich and glamorous could afford the drug.

Evidence of cocaine abuse also emerged from the Institute's Drug Abuse Warning Network, which measures the health consequences of drug abuse by counting the incidence of medical emergencies and deaths caused by drugs. In 1981 the number of emergency room visits attributed to cocaine was approximately 3,000, but by 1985 this number had more than tripled to 10,000 cocaine-related episodes. At the same time, media coverage about the drug experiences of John Belushi, Richard Pryor, and sports celebrities illustrated how cocaine could cause the loss of one's career, health, and life.

Basic pharmacological research and applied treatment research reported in the drug abuse community during the early to mid 1980s also raised concern about the addictive nature of cocaine. Studies showed that, with an unlimited supply of the drug, animals would self-administer cocaine compulsively until death from starvation or seizure. The action of cocaine on the pleasure centers of the brain provided an initial understanding of the powerfully reinforcing nature of the drug. Cocaine's pharmacological effects on the brain explained health consequences such as strokes, seizures, and heart attacks, which had earlier been reported as resulting from cocaine use.

The knowledge and attitudes about cocaine use held by the general public during the late 1970s and the early 1980s were consistent with the increased popularity of the drug. Cocaine was generally viewed, even by some members of the drug abuse treatment and research communities, as a nonaddictive, relatively safe "recreational drug." It was reputed to be the glamour drug of the 1980s. Its use was glamorized and promoted in films, television, and popular music as the "thing to do" and with the promise that its use would improve and enhance one's ability to perform and have fun: Want a lift? Need that extra competitive edge? Want better sex? Cocaine will provide it. It does all of the work. All you do is enjoy.

THE GROUNDWORK – "JUST SAY NO"

Planning for NIDA's national media cocaine prevention campaign began in June 1984. The Institute's Communications Services Branch, now the Office for Research Communications, had demonstrated that it could engage and enlist the national media in the service of drug abuse prevention. The "Just Say No" campaign, aimed at young teenagers and their parents, was in its second year. Radio and television public service announcements, a creative music video, print ads, posters, and brochures reached millions of teenagers and their parents. The slogan, "Just Say No," became the national rallying cry for drug abuse prevention, thanks to the work of First Lady Nancy Reagan, members of the national parents movement, and others dedicated to preventing drug abuse among the nation's youth.

The efforts of these people at the local level to address the issue of kids and drugs made drug abuse among the nation's youth an item of vital community importance. Members of community groups were available to assist NIDA staff in marketing campaign materials to local radio and television station managers and to newspaper editors. This citizen involvement ensured that there would be an audience core who was willing to hear NIDA's message and to promote it to others. As a result, response to the "Just Say No" public service announcements was so favorable that the ads were still running when this book went to press—more than 3 years after they were first released.

Another important factor in the success of the "Just Say No" campaign was the credibility and usefulness of the information it communicated. The ads told teenagers and their parents, in a factual manner, that drug use has important consequences for them and their families. Peer pressure was addressed directly, and the ads gave teens helpful, supportive advice on how to deal with it.

DEVELOPING THE CAMPAIGN AGAINST COCAINE

Armed with the initial experience and success, NIDA staff was ready to try the same approach in addressing the national problem of cocaine abuse. The communication strategy for cocaine abuse prevention was designed to increase public awareness of the serious social and health consequences of cocaine use. The campaign countered myths about the safety and glamour of cocaine by presenting credible, useful information in a manner that would reach and hold the attention of the target audience.

NIDA staff launched its strategy with the release of two monographs, produced by NIDA researchers, on the pharmacology and treatment of cocaine use. The monographs were followed with the release of reports in the popular press about NIDA-funded research that demonstrated the reinforcing addictive nature of cocaine. The staff also produced and widely distributed a public information booklet called *Cocaine Addiction: It Costs Too Much.*

Work on the campaign itself began when NIDA signed a contract with the Advertising Council in July 1985. The Ad Council, a voluntary organization of advertising agencies and media corporations, helps organizations produce and distribute national media campaigns. The council solicited the voluntary creative services of Needham Harper Worldwide for the cocaine campaign—the same agency that had helped create the "Just Say No" campaign. Because materials were aired as a public service, costs could be limited to production and distribution. The Ad Council also lends its expertise and guidance in campaign development and helps influence the media to ensure campaign exposure.

NIDA's task was to thoroughly educate the ad agency's creative team about the problem of cocaine abuse. NIDA staff members worked closely with the agency's creative staff for the first 3 months of the contract to ensure that the agency understood the facts and NIDA's principal concerns. The briefings included a review of the research and treatment literature, meetings with epidemiologists and drug treatment experts, interviews with cocaine users and rehabilitated addicts, and focus group sessions with members of potential target audiences.

As the briefings continued, it became clear that the primary target audiences should include young adult cocaine users, potential cocaine users, and their "significant others" (immediate family and friends). Research had shown that a sizable number of 18- to 25-year-olds were using cocaine regularly and that even more were "dabbling" and showed sustained interest in the drug. Potential users were defined as regular users of marijuana who had a strong curiosity about cocaine. These individuals revealed in focus groups that they identified with recreational cocaine users who seemed to benefit from the drug. Many hoped to afford their own cocaine in the future.

The concept of empowering significant others to influence cocaine users and those at risk was a carry-over from the "Just Say No" campaign, in which parents and teachers were identified as a natural group to reinforce and support the prevention message directed at teenagers. NIDA staff wanted similar "allies" in the cocaine abuse prevention campaign, but was not sure initially who such allies would be. Unlike teenagers, young adults are nominally independent of control by others. Because focus group research showed the importance of work to young adults, even to those using cocaine, the employer was considered as an ally. The nation's business community was already concerned about drugs in the workplace because of effects on productivity and insurance costs. NIDA's advertisements for the business press were aimed at teaching employers how to deal constructively with cocaine-using employees. This aspect of the campaign eventually developed independently to become a major NIDA initiative on drugs in the workplace.

Reaching the young adult audience was a challenge for NIDA and the creative team. They were to conduct an intervention campaign with a hard-to-reach audience who more than likely did not want to hear the message. The campaign staff knew that members of the target audience viewed themselves as sophisticated, independent adults who knew everything they needed to know about cocaine. The target audience was eventually conceptualized as knowing all of the positives about cocaine—its social acceptability, high status, "harmlessness"—but unaware of the negatives. The main challenge of the campaign was to give target audience members reasons for not using cocaine and to direct them to help if they wanted it.

The creative strategy was simply to communicate this message: Cocaine is extremely addictive and causes severe social, medical, and psychiatric problems. The slogan "Cocaine, The Big Lie" challenged the beliefs and attitudes commonly held about cocaine and its promises.

The first series of public service announcements featured ex-users. It was produced in January 1986 and was first aired in April 1986. Figure 3.1 shows print versions of two of these ads. Later in that year an additional group of television public service announcements were produced featuring three nonusers of cocaine—major league baseball stars Michael Schmidt and Reggie Jackson, as well as First Lady Nancy Reagan. Their messages both told nonusers to avoid trying cocaine and appealed to users to get help.

A total of 13 public service announcements were produced for the "Cocaine, The Big Lie" campaign, and these were very well received by the media. NIDA monitored the number of times that "Cocaine, The Big Lie" public service announcements were aired during the first year of the campaign. Broadcast Advertisers Reports, Inc., reported that the number of plays within 75 local television markets ranged from 1,500 to 2,500 per month. Such wide exposure is most unusual for a government-sponsored public service campaign; by comparison, the "Just Say No" public service announcements played only 1,150 times per month at their peak.

NIDA's success in getting out the cocaine abuse prevention message is due in part to the quality of the public service announcements, which have won prizes at the American Film and Video Festival and have been entered in other competitions. The currency of the campaign also contributed to its success. The campaign built on the already-focusing public attention on cocaine abuse, and the NIDA public service announcements were the first available on the subject. The ad's topicality also appealed to television station public service directors, who are most likely to air public service announcements that deal with subjects of concern to their local communities.

By the summer of 1986 cocaine was an important item on the national

MERCURY MORRIS
AND THEN I GOT BUSTED.
There was this guy, a nationally known sports hero. And then I got busted. As a result of my lust for cocaine, I bypassed high and went straight to messed up. I mean zoom—there was no stopping. Some of you know exactly what I'm talking about because you're taking the exact same ride. A phone call could help you. It took prison to help me.
COCAINE. THE BIG LIE. CALL 1-800-662-HELP.
TOM M.
I STOLE FOR COCAINE.
See, cocaine torments you 'til you'll do anything to get it. You become evil; a real conniver. I'm not that bad a guy. I'm not that low. When you do cocaine you lie to yourself about being in control. I got to the point where my life was going down the drain and I didn't even care. Anyone tells you cocaine's ok—don't believe it.
COCAINE. THE BIG LIE. CALL 1-800-662-HELP.

FIG. 3.1.

agenda. In addition to the NIDA campaign, the tragic death from a cocaine overdose of University of Maryland basketball star Len Bias, the continuing revelations of cocaine use by professional athletes, and the advent of crack cocaine focused intense media and governmental attention on cocaine abuse during the last half of that year.

TOLL-FREE DRUG TREATMENT REFERRAL LINE

Another important feature of the cocaine abuse-prevention campaign's success is the toll-free telephone number for callers to learn about local treatment programs. In creating the campaign, NIDA staff members were strongly urged by their advisory group and creative team to offer users more than just a message to stop using cocaine. Cocaine users need help to stop; directing them to treatment programs would provide an invaluable service. It would also put NIDA staff in direct contact with users, allowing them to learn more about users' problems first hand and to give users more personally tailored information about cocaine use than any public service announcement could provide.

Staff members working on 1-800-662-HELP responded to more than 50,000 callers in the line's first year of operation. Its staffing and hours of operation had to grow considerably during the first year in order to keep with caller demand, which initially averaged about 1,000 calls received per month when the line was staffed only 40 hours a week by two full-time equivalent staff members. When this book went to press, the referral line was responding to more than 6,000 calls per month with 13 full-time equivalent staff members covering the line 18 hours per day, 7 days a week.

The major purpose of the referral line is to provide information about cocaine use, its consequences, and treatment. Typical questions include: How can you tell if someone is using? What does cocaine do to your body? What do you mean by addiction – is it psychological or physical? How can I convince my spouse (child, or friend) to stop using? How do you feel when you try to stop? What is treatment like? Is it guaranteed to work or is it up to the person? How much does it cost?

Written information is sent if the caller wants it. Often callers want to become well informed before taking a course of action involving themselves or others. NIDA staff send booklets, fact sheets, and reproduced articles to approximately 200 callers per day.

Treatment information details local programs where callers can seek direct help. Staff members are prepared to discuss different treatment approaches, costs, location, insurance coverage, confidentiality, and other concerns. Referral line staff members also connect users and significant others with support groups such as Cocaine Anonymous, Narcotics Anonymous, Nar-Anon, Coke-Anon, local crisis hotlines, local and state treatment referral lines, and state drug abuse offices for additional referrals.

Perhaps the most important function served by the hotline is the confidential human contact provided to people in great distress because of cocaine. Such contact can make all of the difference in getting help.

In summary, the "Cocaine, The Big Lie" campaign used the media to provide information aimed at affecting the public's view of cocaine use, including information aimed at preventing use. Although there is no way of knowing how much cocaine use has been prevented by the campaign, the heavy response to the referral hotline indicates that the campaign is a success.

4

National Media Coverage of Drug Issues, 1983–1987

John E. Merriam
Conference on Issues & Media

National media coverage of drug issues between 1983 and 1987 followed a classic pattern: There was a slow initial increase in overall media attention, followed by a shift in emphasis to subject matters of broader interest. Then interest in drugs increased sharply, peaked, and declined.

The pattern is classic, because it is similar to the track set by many other issues: There was a distinct opening, peak, and decline. There were some differences in the way the drug abuse issue emerged, however, because the national drug issue was subject to unusually strong public information campaigns from the National Institute on Drug Abuse and was exploited to some extent by politicians in 1986 as national elections approached.

These influences, which would by themselves have led to a sharp peaking of media interest, were accentuated by other events, most notably the tragic death due to cocaine overdose of Maryland basketball star Len Bias early in the summer of 1986. Bias' death posed an almost media-perfect example of the dangers of drug overdose to a successful role model for youth. Concern for his death matched closely with the concerns national media and government leaders were seeking to present.

One of the most interesting characteristics of the diffusion of the drug story among the national media between 1983 and 1987 was the way the coverage sharply peaked in 1986 and then sharply declined. Was this the result of overexposure and overreaction, a slackening of drug education efforts, or competition with other more pressing media stories? Or were there factors connected with the way the peak occurred that led to its sharp decline? Matching the peak in drug coverage against coverage of other issues that we have followed at the Conference on Issues & Media over the past 5 years suggests that the way the drug "story" developed contributed to its decline.

In addition, the nature of the drug issue and its ability to transform itself into many subissues suggest that the 1986 peak might be only the first of a series of peaks over several years. Issues expressed through the mass media tend to rise to a peak in coverage, gain some kind of settlement in terms of consensus, and then either reform or spin off into other areas. Continuing drug coverage, at a low level in the national media and at a somewhat higher level in the local media, will work toward a reappearance of the drug problem as a major issue. Impetus for the re-emergence could come from the arrival of new drug types or from increased emphasis on drugs from national leaders, particularly elected officials.

TRACKING DRUG ISSUES

The National Media Index assesses the relative amount of time and space devoted to issues in successive 2-week periods. Each issue is given a rating that expresses its coverage as a percentage of the space and time devoted to all issues during the 2 weeks. Data from television, news magazines, and newspapers are aggregated within each medium and weighted according to where Americans prefer to get their national news. The weights are derived from survey data on how Americans with college-entry level education seek information on public issues. The work of Dr. Robert T. Bower, of the Bureau of Social Sciences Research, Washington, DC, shows that this group draws its information in the following ratios: television–6, newspapers–4, and magazines–3. Drug issues are a subset of the major category "social" news and are classified as subissues of "crime" and of "substance abuse."

The index includes the measurement of time devoted to issues in the evening news broadcasts of ABC, CBS, and NBC networks, as well as weighted space counts from *Newsweek, Time,* and *U.S. News & World Report* and from the *Chicago Tribune, The Los Angeles Times, The New York Times, The Wall Street Journal,* and *The Washington Post.* These 11 media are used as proxies for all national news sources. Numbers are presented as a percentage of the total space time available to these media and devoted to any given subject.

THE CHANGING COVERAGE OF DRUGS

Figure 4.1 shows changes in national media coverage of (a) all drug issues, (b) drug crimes and trafficking, and (c) drug abuse.

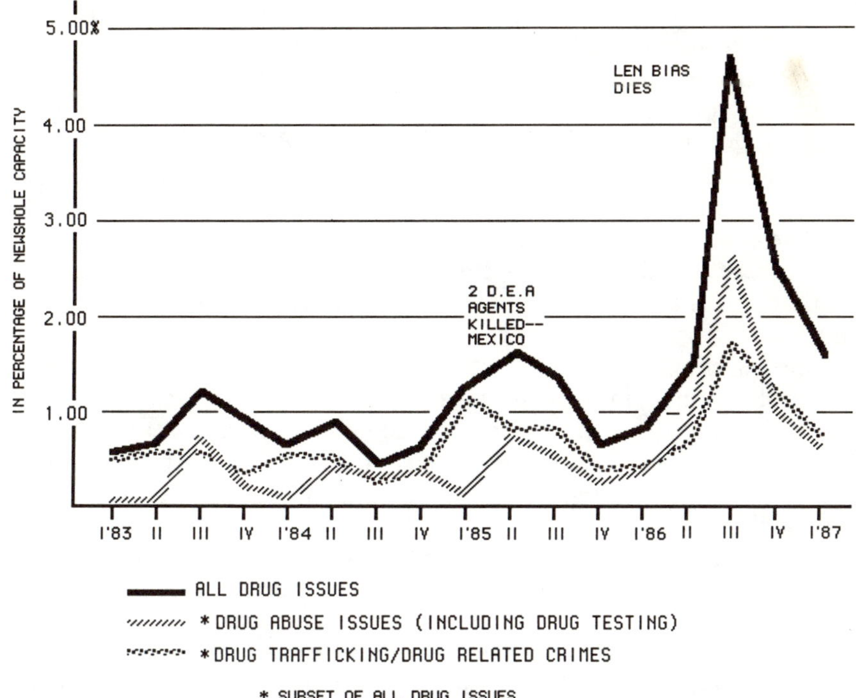

FIG. 4.1   Coverage of drug issues in the national media, 1982–1987.
© Copyright 1987 by The Conference on Issues & Media, Inc., Alexandria, VA.

In the early 1980s, drugs were already a significant issue in the national media, accounting for about 1% of the total national coverage in C.I.M.'s National Media Index–roughly equivalent to 10,000 inches of print coverage in major newspapers around the country or about 15 minutes of evening network news in a 2-week period. By the last half of 1983, drug issues were getting this kind of attention continuously.

But the focus in 1983 was not on drug abuse so much as on drug crimes, including drug trafficking, drug busts, and prevention efforts. Coverage in 1984 was not much different; the exposure of drug abuse did not rise noticeably, and in fact, coverage of all drug issues was down for the year. It is worth noting that, although 1984 was a Presidential election year in which the incumbent had a strong interest in drugs, the issue was not the subject of great attention in the campaign. Other issues, especially social equity problems (including civil rights and the homeless) got markedly increased media attention over the year, as might be expected at election time. Drug abuse was not a politically contentious issue in 1984, but 1985 was different.

Total national media coverage of all drug issues over the year was roughly 80% higher in 1985 than in the previous year. The portion of media attention to drug abuse as compared with drug trafficking and crimes rose appreciably. Two significant events stimulated media coverage of drugs—the loss of a Drug Enforcement Administration agent in Mexico and the emergence of "crack," a new form of cocaine. As Figure 4.1 shows, 1985 coverage was the foothill for the mountain of drug coverage that was to come. In 1985 the media emphasized the dangers of drugs almost as much as they emphasized the overall issue of environmental poisons and life-threatening diseases, including AIDS.

In 1986 a number of forces came together to produce a substantial rise in national drug coverage. First-quarter coverage was not noticeably different from that of the previous year, but then the National Institute on Drug Abuse's phrase "Just Say No" seemed to catch on. The national media began to look seriously at the idea that changes in attitudes toward drugs might be occurring. It was also at this time that media focused on the arrival of "crack."

The slogan "Just Say No" was well attuned to the climate of opinion on drugs. Increased fear of the negative effects of drugs was stimulated by the introduction of crack, and this fear fed a trend that had already begun toward conservative social behavior in American society. This conservative social trend had been evident for some time in the major media's increasing focus on morality issues, including heavier attention to pornography, drunk driving (which had previously peaked in 1983), issues related to sexual behavior, and religion.

The debate over drugs grew to national proportions in the second quarter of 1986 as the White House became more active. It soon became apparent to Democrats in Congress that drug abuse could be a major political asset to their opposition. Democrats began to compete for attention on the drug issue, being well aware that the White House had successfully used issues such as the balanced budget amendment and abortion to rally the GOP faithful during the 1982 off-year election. The Democrats quickly joined the drug issue, forming a bipartisan political consensus and thus forestalling use of the drug issue against them. By the time the White House declared its "war on drugs" in late summer 1986, there was common agreement on the evil.

The peak came in the third quarter of 1986, which opened in the immediate aftermath of the sudden death of Maryland basketball star Len Bias in June 1986. Four weeks after his death, national coverage of drug abuse accounted for 3.2% of all coverage. It had become a top issue, but still ranked ninth in order of exposure behind the Statue of Liberty celebration (12.3%), general worries over money and credit (4.9%), health (4.3%), morality issues (4%), immigration (3.9%), and South Africa (3.8%).

Len Bias' death brought together the political and human aspects of drug abuse. His death accentuated the attention placed on drugs after the announcement of the "war on drugs." Although consensus about the need to "do something" was generally accepted, politicians continued to argue over the best approach – whether to spend Federal money or rely on private efforts.

From August through October 1986, the "war on drugs" captured a significant share of the national media's attention. The issue played almost like a campaign question, but, because there was very little contention, it appeared to have little meaning for the elections. As a consequence, the uptrend in coverage turned down after the White House declared the "war" in August 1986. Drug coverage peaked at 6% of all media coverage in the 2 weeks ending August 10. By November 5, coverage of all drug issues had fallen to 2.9%.

The decline continued for months afterward, although in the fourth quarter of 1986 drug coverage still accounted for a respectable 2.4% of all coverage. By the first quarter of 1987, drug coverage had declined to 1.1% of all coverage, but this was well ahead of the previous year.

THE ROLE OF TELEVISION

Figure 4.2 compares overall media coverage of drugs with that from the ABC, CBS, and NBC evening television newscasts. The figure shows that, although the three television networks contributed to a fairly constant proportion of the total amount of media's drug coverage, they lagged slightly behind the print media in moving drug coverage to its peak. Figure 4.2 shows that overall media coverage of drugs began increasing during the second quarter of 1986, well ahead of network television. This is not surprising, because television frequently seems to use print media as its memory and archive and thus as its precursor. National television news is often a lag indicator, in spite of very recent efforts to speed coverage of fast-breaking regional and local news into the network's evening shows.

In addition, television is a "hot" medium – more likely to be dependent on news events rather than on opinion or commentary. This means that television will also be quicker to leave a major story like the "war on drugs."

ISSUE COMPETITION

With a limited amount of time and space available for news each day in the media, issues find themselves in competition with one another for media attention. By 1987, the media had apparently concluded that drug

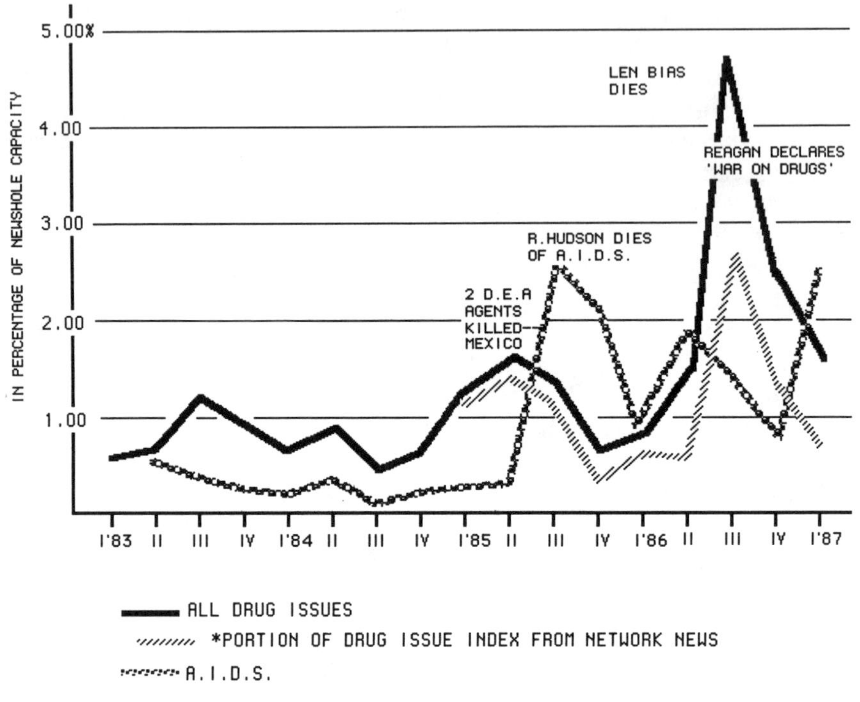

FIG. 4.2   Special aspects of the drug issue – national media coverage 1983–1987.
© Copyright 1987 by The Conference on Issues & Media, Inc., Alexandria, VA.

abuse was less newsworthy than competing issues like the spread of
AIDS. Figure 4.2 shows that, as media coverage of drugs decreased during
late 1986 and early 1987, coverage of AIDS increased. A similar pattern
had also occurred in 1985, when actor Rock Hudson's death due to AIDS
apparently caused a dramatic increase in media coverage of AIDS and a
substantial decrease in drug coverage.

The nature of the drug abuse news stories may also have contributed to
the drug issue's demise. Drug abuse is also an "up close" issue that may be
more appropriate for local news media than for national coverage. Local
media have traditionally given individual crimes more news space and
time than have the national media. As a consequence of this local
orientation to most of the drug news, the national media tended to move
in and out of the issue instead of giving it sustained attention. The drug
issue seemed to lack week-in, week-out staying power in the absence of
events like the death of Len Bias that capture the public's imagination.
Drug "busts" and abuse involving public figures still could get the national
media's attention in early 1987, especially that of sportswriters, but there

was still no evidence that drug scandals were playing a growing role in national news.

It is important to remember that national news is only a portion of the news diet regularly received by Americans. Local and regional news are also important, particularly with an issue like drug abuse that closely touches family life. Local television news offers strong coverage of crime involving drugs as well as drug abuse. The networks' interest in drugs would probably diminish if national news managers assume that a certain amount of coverage is already getting through via local channels.

Another factor limiting the coverage of drugs in the national media is that, unlike other issues such as nuclear safety, ozone depletion, or AIDS, the drug issue seems to lack futurity. There is little sense of the inevitable in media coverage of drug abuse. Media suggest that children will be tainted, but the final picture of devastation is somehow not part of the story. The media stopped short of predictions about country-wide, inev-

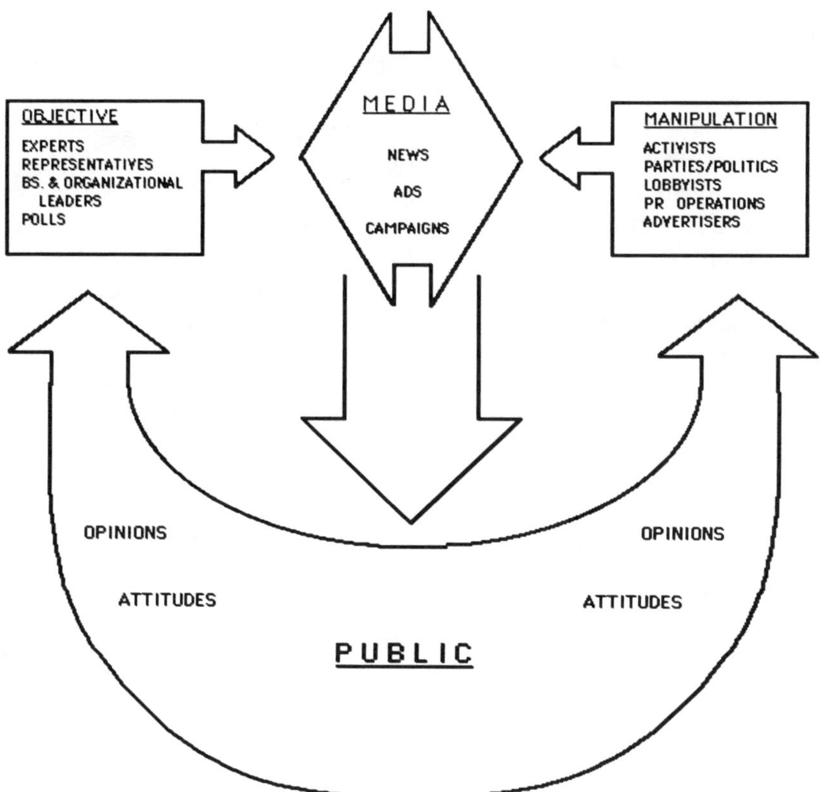

FIG. 4.3 Newsflow—a continuous information exchange.
© Copyright 1987 by The Conference on Issues & Media, Inc., Alexandria, VA.

itable devastation due to drugs. Without this ability to convey doom, the drug abuse story will inevitably lack staying power when it must compete with other issues for news coverage.

THE FUTURE OF DRUG COVERAGE

The drug story can easily, and probably will, return again and again to national media news. But it is unlikely that the level of media intensity reached in 1986 will return unless (a) the ravages of widespread drug use can be more clearly shown to the public; (b) public attitudes, which have allowed a certain tolerance, change more than they have; or (c) a more coordinated and massive attack than has yet appeared is mounted by both public and private groups. Too often in recent years, the drug problem has been treated symbolically by national leaders. The cynicism associated with exploiting issues in this way communicates quickly to the working press. As a consequence, coverage of the drug issue has been sometimes thoughtful, sometimes superficial.

In this way, the media have reflected the public's attitude at large. In the business of producing and selling news, large media organizations are generally in the business of reporting back to the public what it needs to know and is willing to pay for (see Fig. 4.3). The management skill of news organizations is to be able to recognize stories that fit this test. Drug issues have generally ranked fairly well, but they have not proved as durable as many people, knowing the seriousness of the problem, would like them to be.

5

Intermedia Influence and the Drug Issue: Converging on Cocaine

Stephen D. Reese
Lucig H. Danielian
University of Texas at Austin

> *In recent weeks, as the intense attention to drugs has faded, some have asked if the reaction to drugs was appropriate, and how it is that the press and Congress sometimes suddenly discover and then dismiss a major national problem.*
>
> —Kerr, 1986, p.1

Kerr was talking about drug coverage in the media, but the same could be said for many other national issues that rise and fall in prominence with each passing month. Many issues, such as the nuclear threat and the national debt, endure from year to year, but others seem more fleeting.

Big events drive many big stories and draw general attention to the problems they represent. Rock Hudson's death spurred national attention to the AIDS crisis. Spy arrests led to other questions about the quality of national security safeguards, and three major airline crashes in 1985 produced a rash of stories on air safety.

Other stories are less tied to specific events yet become big nevertheless. In the last couple of years such stories have included the famine in Ethiopia, Mideast terrorism, and the farm crisis. The problems behind these stories existed before the media "found" them and continued to exist after attention waned.

Each of these stories was characterized by a rapid convergence of media attention, during which it seemed that all media channels as well as conversations on the street are filled with the story. Although this bandwagon tendency among the media is not new in the press, one wonders if it has become more pronounced in recent times. This study is a first attempt to explore what is now a rather impressionistic notion of how the big media converge on a big story, especially those not directly tied to big events. The drug issue, particularly the "cocaine summer" of 1986, is a perfect example of such an issue and one explored in depth in this chapter and the next. Lacking any objective evidence of a drug epidemic or crisis (Kerr, 1986), we must look to the media themselves to determine why the drug issue received such a concentrated amount of coverage in such a short time. Such a systematic analysis is required before we can say much more about the impressionistic and anecdotal notion of media "convergence." Convergence may be considered the observed manifest similarities in media coverage – in timing, emphasis, and source selection. Several interrelated processes underlie this convergence, including intermedia influence.[1]

MANY MEDIA, FEW VOICES

For many stories, convergence of media coverage may be harmless – a natural result of organizations covering the same "reality." Similarities in coverage may simply result from equally accurate news judgments. If convergence occurs in stories that are not purely event-driven, however, media organizations may be looking to each other for guidance in an ambiguous situation (as, we argue, was the case for the drug issue). It has been suggested that, because the drug issue (particularly crack and cocaine) was a problem for New York City, it became a problem for the rest of the country by virtue of the coverage received in papers like *The New York Times.*

Although perhaps functional for the organizations themselves, such a tendency to follow the leader and each other could have serious societal implications. Too much sameness in media content conflicts with a key

---

[1]The concept of intermedia "convergence" is introduced here, although in the next chapter the term *intermedia agenda setting* is also used. Convergence better describes a process whereby the media discover issues, respond to each other in a cycle of peaking coverage, before largely dismissing the issues. This narrower term is preferred initially because the agenda-setting metaphor has come to be used so broadly that it might describe almost any influence process having to do with prioritizing public issues. Agenda setting may more properly describe the day-to-day cross-checking of story lineups that newsworkers engage in to check their decisions about the relative emphasis to be given various issues. Also, as a methodological distinction, we look at a single "story" here rather than an "agenda" of issues, and do not conceive the process as necessarily an orderly transmission of "saliences," implying a relatively greater attention to some issues at the expense of others. Finally, we eventually hope to go beyond examining not only the quantity of attention given an "issue," as most agenda-setting studies have done. Indeed, our main concern is the extent to which the media converge, not only on similar topics, but also similar themes, interpretations, and sources.

value of American pluralistic society, that the press should present a diverse set of views and voices.

In recent years, technological advances have helped expand the number of available channels of information for the audience and enhanced the ability of news organizations to cover stories, but it is not clear whether this has done anything to diversify content. There may be more newsworkers now than 15 years ago (Weaver & Wilhoit, 1986), but they do little to further diversity if they all cover the "big" stories. Parenti (1986), for example, noted that the few Washington journalists working for progressive publications run into virtually no competition from the mainstream press corps in seeking their stories. In addition, the sheer volume of attention generated when the national press converges on a story, like drugs, virtually demands a political response. In their haste, these reactions may not always be carefully considered (a charge many leveled at the Congressional antidrug initiative in the fall of 1986).

COCAINE MEDIA HYPE

Although the mainstream news media routinely tend to cover the same stories, some stories are tackled with a vengeance. What critics call media "hype" is a visible manifestation of this phenomenon of intermedia convergence. As for the drug issue itself, Edwin Diamond (1987) and his News Study Group at New York University noted that by August 1986, television had begun to reflect on its drug coverage over the summer, questioning whether it had been exaggerated, and media treatment of cocaine became a story itself. Nevertheless, high-profile television coverage continued through early September 1986 with a CBS documentary, "48 Hours on Crack Street," on September 2, and NBC's "Cocaine Country," aired on September 5. Perhaps in response, on September 23, PBS's McNeil/Lehrer Newshour featured a lengthy discussion (22 minutes) on whether the drug problem was hyped by the media.[2]

No one would accuse the media of "hyping" a story if first one paper examined a story, then another, and so on. But when every news organization emphasizes the same story at roughly the same time in a "feeding frenzy," the amount of coverage often seems out of proportion to the problem at hand. ABC reporter John Quinones confirmed that this was the case with the drug issue in 1986, noting that "sometimes we [the

---

[2]Other less mainstream media have also noted the exaggerated coverage given the drug issue. Hatch (1987), for example, characterized the drug "hype" as a carefully orchestrated disinformation campaign promulgated by the Reagan administration to help pursue attacks on domestic freedoms and mask more pressing social problems. Indeed, any number of intrusive drug testing programs have been advocated in the aftermath of the drug summer of 1986.

media] have a tendency to feed on one another, and the story feeds upon itself" (Diamond, 1987, p. 10).

The drug issue is a good example of a big story that may have been blown out of proportion by the media. For one thing, the story seemed to have a distinct rise and fall of media attention. It fits our notion of media convergence and allows for relatively easy definition and measurement. In addition, any similarities in media coverage of drugs cannot be explained by "pack journalism." The story did not emerge from a special "beat," as do national political stories. The nature of pack journalism on these beats is familiar by now. If several organizations assign reporters to cover the same thing, the resulting coverage tends necessarily to be similar. It deals with similar events and is filtered through the standardizing influence of the pack.

Although specific events, like the death of Len Bias, did drive some media coverage, the drug issue was not covered by packs nor confined to a specific geographical location. Key editorial decisions were made to give greater treatment to the issue and these decisions were observed by others in the media. Furthermore, the story was not promoted by any one party, candidate, agency, or group. Rather, drugs have been a problem for years, but only recently was a significant convergence of coverage observed.

This study examines what was in many ways a media-created issue and uses that issue to compare coverage across media. That coverage may help to shed some light on the process of media convergence by providing evidence of similarities and sequences of coverage.

BACKGROUND

Elite media leadership has not been the subject of much research. No content analysis studies were found that systematically examined the extent of elite media leadership at the national level, and only one study was found below the national level. At the state level, newspapers tended to influence the broadcast agenda for statehouse stories more than the reverse (Atwater, Fico, & Pizante, 1987). Most such research, however, has examined cross-sections of content from different media and found strong similarities (sometimes called "homogeneity," "consonance," or "conformity") in their respective agendas. Newspapers have been compared and found to be similar in the topics covered and in how those topics were treated (e.g., Bigman, 1948; Donohue & Glasser, 1978; Riffe & Shaw, 1982).

Network newscasts have attracted greater attention, and their respective agendas have been found to be very similar (Altheide, 1982; Buckalew, 1969; Capo, 1983; Dominick, 1981; Foote & Steele, 1986;

Fowler & Showalter, 1974; Graber, 1971; Hester, 1978; Lemert, 1974; Meeske & Javaheri, 1982; Riffe, Ellis, Rogers, Van Ommeren, & Woodman, 1986; Stempel & Windhauser, 1984; Weaver, Porter, & Evans, 1984). More than any three newspapers, the network newscasts are functionally equivalent, to the extent that Altheide (1982) declared them a national news service.

The original agenda-setting study by McCombs and Shaw (1972) is one of the few studies to compare agendas across media. Comparing agreement on campaign issue coverage by *The New York Times, Time, Newsweek,* NBC, CBS, and four local newspapers showed a high degree of agreement across those media. These similarities have been variously explained as resulting from similar real-world events, standardized organizational structure, and similar journalist socialization experiences. These explanations do not require that news organizations know what the others are doing. They could operate independently of each other and produce similar content. All of these factors no doubt play a part, but another equally important influence on intermedia agreement is the leadership exerted by some news organizations over others. This explanation obviously does require that the newsworkers know what others are doing.

Others have looked at the relationships among the mass media through case studies and participant observation. Media sociologists have documented an intermedia influence phenomenon, making it clear that looking to other media organizations for confirmation of news judgment is an institutionalized practice. Warren Breed (1980), in his classic study of the newsroom, found evidence that suggested this intermedia leadership process. He termed the phenomenon of one newspaper leading others as "dendritic" influence: "The influence goes 'down' from larger papers to smaller ones, as if the editor of the smaller paper is employing, in absentia, the editors of the larger paper to 'make up' his page for him" (p. 195). This pattern of influence, he said, assumed a dendritic or arterial form with the flow of influence from larger papers to smaller ones. Larger papers weren't copied, but their decisions as to the value of certain stories were followed.

This tendency for newsworkers to look to each other for guidance has remained in full force in more recent years. In *Deciding What's News,* Herbert Gans (1979, p. 91) noted that, when entertaining story ideas, editors will have already read the *Times* and *Post,* and will be aware of how those papers' editors have ruled on the idea(s) in question. If another paper has carried the story, it has been judged satisfactory, "eliminating the need for an independent decision" (p. 126). Gans noted that this prior publication is also taken as evidence of audience appeal, a particularly important element in "trend stories" (like cocaine). Gans said that when it comes to "trend" stories, "the prudent story suggester waits for another news medium to take the lead, then sells the idea partly on the basis that it has been reported elsewhere" (p. 170).

Until other media are onto a story it may have difficulty emerging, but once they are, a story can build exponentially. In *Reporters and Officials* Leon Sigal (1973) observed the importance of intermedia processes: "The consensible nature of news may even impede the breaking of stories that lack corroboration from opinion-leading newspapers. Once they do break, however, big stories will tend to remain in the news as first one news organization and then another uncovers additional information or a new interpretation" (p. 40).

After a story has reached a "critical mass" it may continue in this way, floating loose from any moorings to actual newsworthy events. Why is it so important for news organizations to look to each other for confirmation of news judgment? Sigal is among others who have noted that adherence to routine channels provides a way of coping with uncertainty. The similarities of newsworkers' stories reassures them that they know the "real news." Following the lead of another organization serves the same function. Consistency is accuracy.

Certain media are followed on certain types of issues because they are thought to have special expertise and resources. Miller (1978; pp. 16–17), for example, noted that *The New York Times* is regarded as the leader for how to treat international stories, *The Washington Post* is looked to for leadership for national domestic issues, and *Rolling Stone* is regarded as the leader for counterculture antiestablishment stories. In a case study analysis, she noted how the *Stone's* coverage of Americans in Mexican prisons triggered national print and television coverage, as other media picked up the lead and attention mushroomed.

Are the networks looked to by other media for guidance? Although intermedia influence has been assumed to always flow from print to electronic media (e.g., Massing, 1984), recent developments may have altered this equation. When Gannett designed its national newspaper, *USA Today,* it was with television in mind. From the shape of the paper dispensers to the colorful graphics, the publication was pitched to an audience of television viewers. This includes using the television networks to help guide story decisions. Prichard (1987) described how a December 1982 story about a man attempting to blow up the Washington Monument was bumped from page 1A of *USA Today,* having been deemed a local story. It was reinstated after Dan Rather led with it on the "CBS Evening News." Now that the nation knew about the story, it had become page 1 material. The broadcast by a major network had given the story a "verification factor."

In general, however, newspapers look to other newspapers, and television networks monitor each other, with certain "bellwethers" being tracked by all on specialized issues. But is there one general standard looked to by all the news media? Gans noted what is widely felt by many observers–that ultimately *The New York Times* is used as the final arbiter of quality and professionalism, across journalistic formats. Indeed, in the often ambiguous world of journalism, "if the *Times* did not exist, it would probably have to be invented" (Gans, 1979, p. 181).

THE CASE OF COCAINE

This study examines coverage by several national media of the drug issue over a period of time to determine the extent to which they converged on the drug issue and whether one medium can be said to have led the others. Specifically, the major elite newspapers are examined: *The New York Times, The Wall Street Journal, The Washington Post, The Los Angeles Times,* and *The Christian Science Monitor.* In addition, two major news magazines are examined–*Time* and *Newsweek*–along with the three major network newscasts from ABC, CBS, and NBC.

If intermedia agenda setting took place in the drug issue, we would expect to find substantial similarities in when the various media gave the issue most attention. The rise and fall in attention would be expected to occur at about the same times. The intermedia leadership explanation for that similarity would be strengthened if rises in one organization's coverage could be seen to precede a rise in another's. Of particular interest is the relationship between print and television news, often criticized as merely following the lead of the elite media (Massing, 1984). Finally, this study determines which of the elite newspapers played the largest role in covering the drug issue.

METHOD

The DIALOG information service was used to electronically access newspaper and magazine data bases containing summaries of stories appearing in 1985 and 1986. Any number of search words could have accessed stories related to the drug issue (e.g., drugs, narcotics, drug abuse). Given that the purpose of this study was not to provide a comprehensive evaluation of drug coverage, it was decided to narrow the scope of the search so as to have a manageable, yet comparable, sample of stories across media. Because cocaine was at the center of the drug issue in 1986, the term *cocaine* was used and it elicited a workable number of stories (listed in Tables 5.1 and 5.2). Bibliographical information and a short story summary were obtained for each "cocaine" story.

A similar search strategy was used in seeking network news stories. The Vanderbilt University Television News Index and Abstracts were obtained and searched for stories indexed under "cocaine." All such stories (identified in the Abstracts with an underlined heading) in 1985 and 1986 were coded for date and length in seconds. The searches resulted in 465 newspaper stories, 231 network news stories, and 44 news magazine stories.

Using the Abstract and DIALOG summaries, each story was coded with high intercoder agreement ($cr = .95$) into one of 10 categories (Table 5.1): (a) deaths of prominent people and events surrounding them; (b) specific crimes involving cocaine, such as trials and arrests; (c) efforts by schools, communities, and national figures to discourage the use of cocaine; (d) general reports on the use and abuse of cocaine and the various medical and social implications; (e) policy responses to the drug problem by national, state and local, international, and private sectors; (f) problems encountered by foreign countries in combating drugs (without reference to direct U.S. involvement); and (g) general drug crisis stories (a category reserved for more extensive reporting on the issue).

TABLE 5.1

Nature of Cocaine Stories in *The New York Times, The Washington Post, The Wall Street Journal, The Los Angeles Times,* and *The Christian Science Monitor*

	Medium				
Story Category	*New York Times*	*Wall St. Journal*	*Wash. Post*	*LA Times*	*Chr. Sci. Monitor*
Deaths	7%	0%	24%	1%	0%
Crime	39	39	28	48	35
Antidrug movement	5	0	3	4	0
Use and abuse	26	39	24	17	30
Policy Response					
National	2	4	3	3	4
State/local	5	0	0	1	0
International	6	9	12	11	17
Private sector	2	4	1	0	0
Foreign	5	4	6	14	9
General crisis	2	0	0	0	4
Total	100%	100%	100%	100%	100%
N	(250)	(23)	(98)	(71)	(23)

TABLE 5.2
Nature of Cocaine Stories Transmitted by the Television Networks and News
Magazines

| | Medium | | | | |
Story Category	ABC	CBS	NBC	Time	Newsweek
Deaths	14%	9%	14%	13%	5%
Crime	37	41	40	26	19
Antidrug movement	3	4	3	4	0
Use and abuse	27	21	24	22	43
Policy Response					
National	17	8	10	13	0
State/local	1	3	1	0	0
International	4	8	5	9	14
Private sector	3	3	6	9	0
Foreign	3	5	5	0	14
General crisis	0	0	0	4	5
Total	100%	100%	100%	100%	100%
N	(70)	(30)	(81)	(23)	(21)

RESULTS AND DISCUSSION

Tables 5.1 and 5.2 show how the stories in our sample broke down into
the study categories, compared by the 11 news sources. These sources are
combined by medium in Table 5.3. The major types of newspaper
cocaine stories were crime and "use and abuse," accounting for 62% of the
total Comparing across the five newspapers shows that the proportions
of coverage are roughly similar. *The Washington Post* featured cocaine
deaths more prominently than the others, due largely to the great amount
of coverage given the death of hometown basketball star Len Bias. Table
5.2 shows a similar pattern. Television newscasts and the news magazines give their greatest coverage of cocaine to crime and use and abuse
stories. Television gives greater attention, however, to deaths and national policy responses. The three networks show more similarity in their
coverage than do the newspapers.

Table 5.3 provides a combined look at the three media. Newspapers,
news magazines, and television newscasts show similar amounts of
coverage in the study categories. The major difference (enough for a
statistically significant chi-square value) was found in the tendency of
newsmagazines to focus less on crime and more on the use and abuse of
cocaine. The week-to-week nature of the newsmagazines' coverage appears to suit them better to more evaluative trend-type stories than to
specific day-to-day crime coverage.

TABLE 5.3
Overall Nature of Cocaine Stories in Newspapers, News Magazines, and
Television Networks

	Medium		
	Newspapers	News Magazines	Television Networks
Deaths	9%	9%	12%
Crime	38	23	39
Antidrug movement	4	2	3
Use and abuse	25	32	24
Policy Response			
National	3	7	6
State/local	3	0	2
International	9	11	6
Private sector	1	5	4
Foreign	7	7	4
General crisis	2	5	0
Total	100%	100%	100%
N	(465)	(44)	(231)

Chi square (18) = 29.9, $p < .05$

Figures 5.1 through 5.4 take a closer look at media coverage over time
by newspapers and the television networks (*The Christian Science Monitor*
gave cocaine relatively little coverage and was omitted from the newspaper comparison charts). During 1985 it does not appear that there was a
distinctive media convergence, but 1986 does show evidence of this
phenomenon. *The New York Times* covered the baseball trials, involving
cocaine use by some Mets players, heavily in August and September
1985. That was largely a local issue, however, and the other papers did
not pay much attention to that story or cocaine generally, until *The Los
Angeles Times* printed a major multipart series at year's end. The network
newscasts showed a similar pattern in 1985. ABC carried the most
coverage early in the year with CBS and NBC picking up the pace later
on. Again, the coverage is diffused, and no internetwork agenda similarity is observed. Great similarities are seen in 1986 where both the volume
and concentration of coverage increased substantially. The peak of coverage shown graphically in Fig. 5.2 and 5.4 in the summer of 1986 hints
at the media convergence phenomenon suggested earlier.

Comparisons among combined media are shown in Fig. 5.5, 5.6, and
5.7. Two different processes are suggested by media coverage in 1985
(Fig. 5.5). One process is the leading of one medium by others. For
example, television stories show a marked rise in March following a
similar increase in the number of *New York Times* and news magazine
stories the month before. February 1985 saw two cover stories in *Time* and

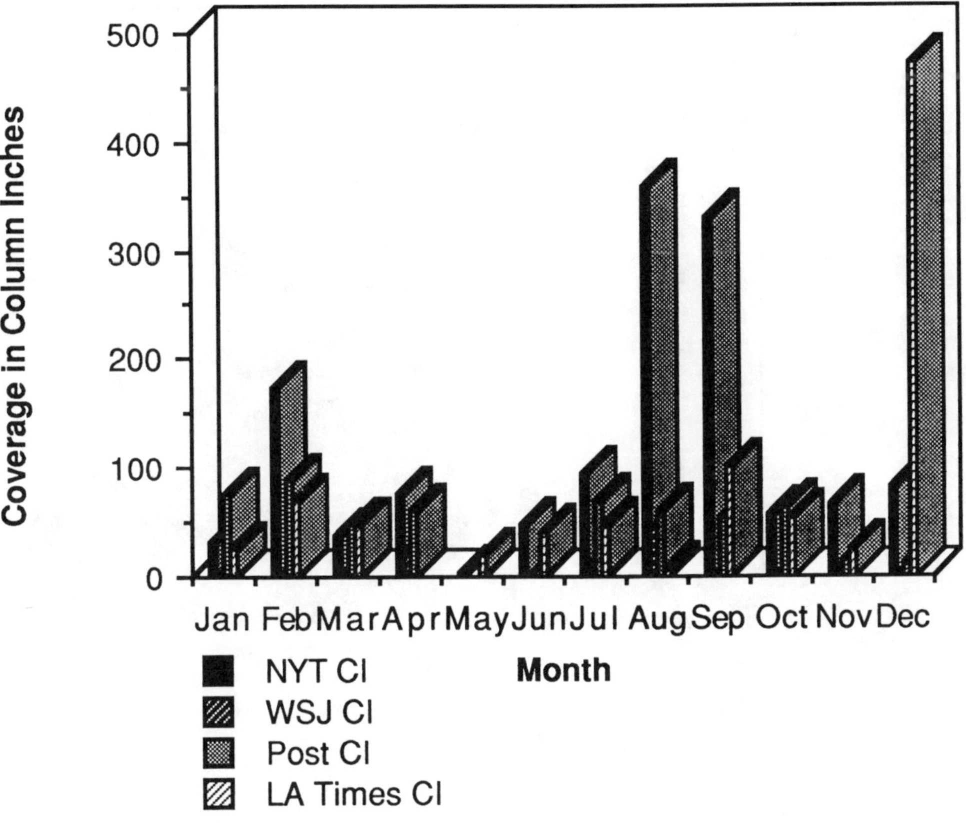

FIG. 5.1.   1985 newspaper coverage of cocaine issues.

Newsweek on cocaine trafficking. The television networks followed this emphasis with stories of their own. Later in the year another process seems to take place. A major event, the baseball drug trials of September, drives the coverage of all three media resulting in a simultaneous peak in coverage.

Figure 5.6 suggests a combination of these processes occurring in 1986. The death of athletes Len Bias and Don Rogers in June of that year drew a significant amount of media attention. But that coverage built on previous attention to the cocaine problem. Evidence for media leadership may be found in the fact that three of New York City's major newspapers carried extensive articles on cocaine and crack on May 18. These stories were followed by a rush of coverage in other media in the following months, climaxing in the peak of media attention seen in July. So although the death of the athletes may be considered prominent events driving each medium's agenda, these events probably had the effect of

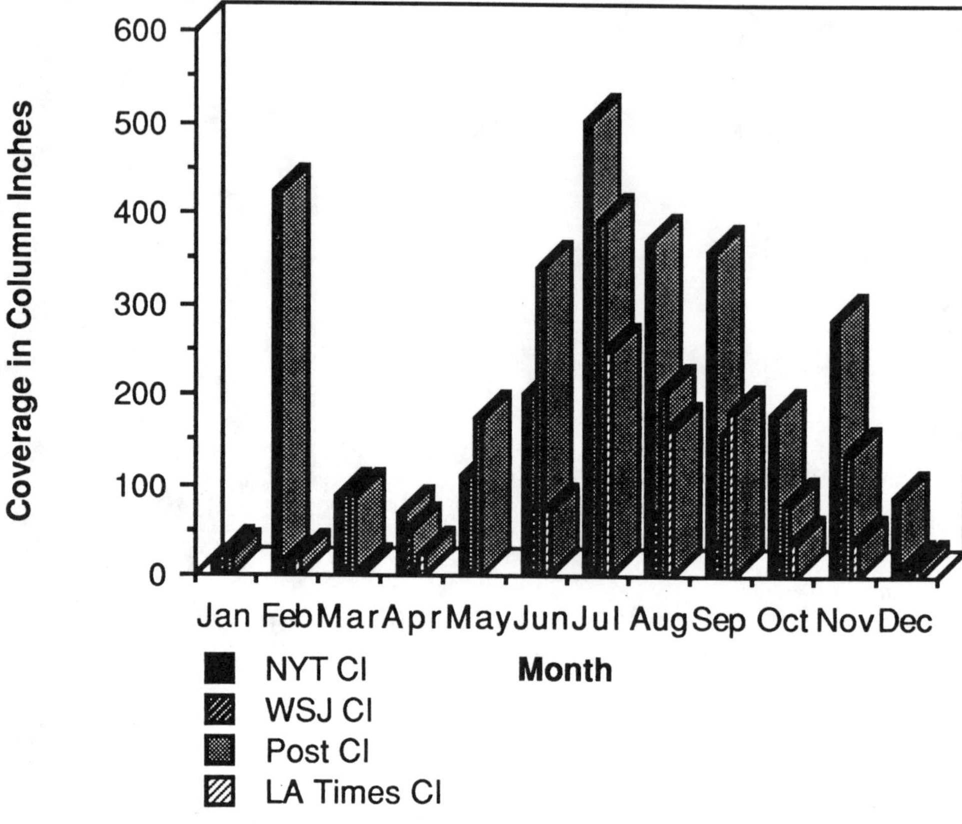

FIG. 5.2.   1986 newspaper coverage of cocaine issues.

focusing press attention on an issue already set in motion. They provided a hook, or newspeg, on which to hang the cocaine story.

Judging from Fig. 5.2, *The New York Times* took the lead in covering the cocaine issue. The other papers quickly fell in line, though, around mid-year. *The Wall Street Journal* was least likely to follow the others, playing the cocaine story up and down throughout the year, with a slight rise in mid-year. The *Journal* has a specialized audience, however, and tended to run cocaine stories when a major business was involved. After the three New York papers covered the crack/cocaine story in the middle of May, the *Post* ran a long "use and abuse" story of its own a few days later. After the *Times* and the *Post* devoted major attention to the issue in June, *The Los Angeles Times* jumped on and stayed with the issue through September. A loose interpretation of Fig. 5.2 suggests that the *Times* laid the groundwork for the story, which gathered strength when the *Post*

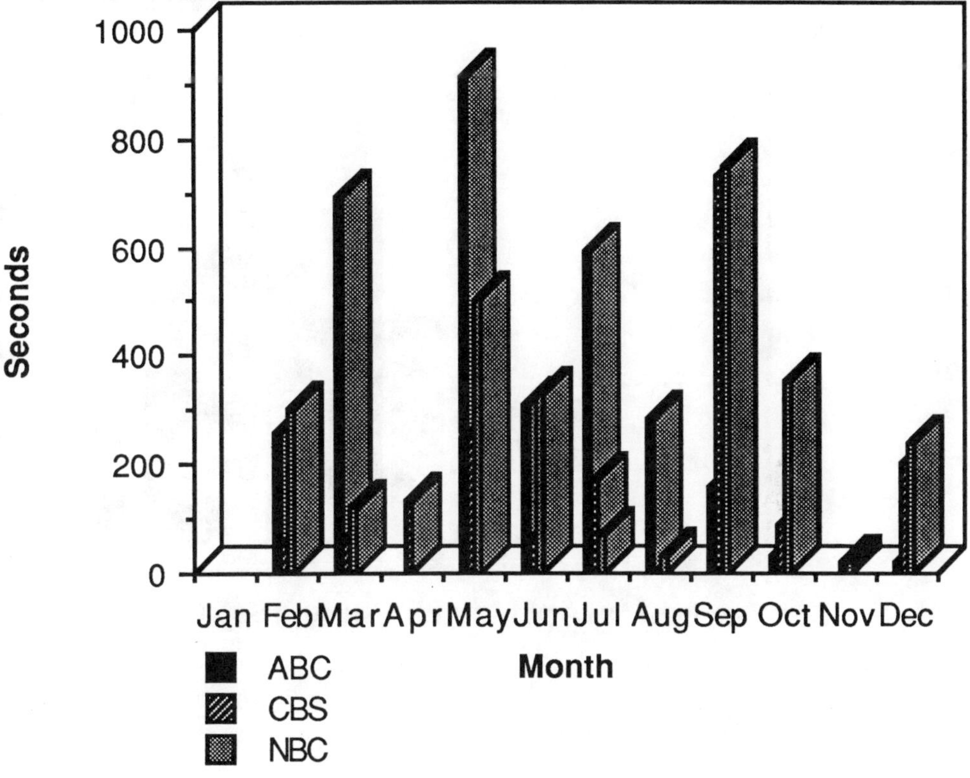

FIG. 5.3. 1985 network news coverage of cocaine issues.

picked up the story and expanded it with a heavy focus on the Len Bias death. With two elite papers running with the story, *The Los Angeles Times* was obliged to join in.

It appears that the print media, and specifically *The New York Times*, set the agenda for the television networks. Network coverage peaked in September with dual documentaries on CBS and NBC on the cocaine problem, while attention by the print media had already begun to wane. This process is seen more clearly in Fig. 5.7, which shows all news stories combined. Interestingly, the television networks dropped the issue completely in December while newspapers continued coverage at a lower level. Television news, more than newspapers, appears to follow a smooth attention curve, discovering an issue, playing it strongly, and then moving on to other stories. This tendency may contribute to the notion that the media converge on issues, resulting in a short national attention span.

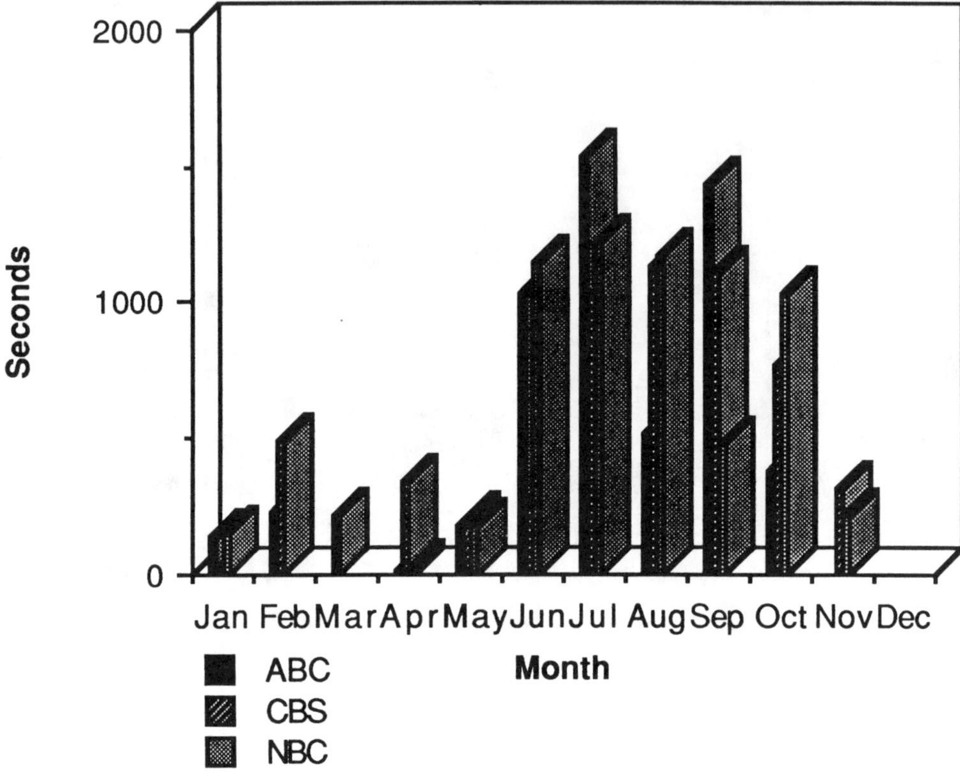

FIG. 5.4.   1986 network news coverage of cocaine issues.

This study has presented a preliminary look at intermedia coverage similarities, and media leadership. The results support the view that the major media cover issues in a similar fashion and at roughly the same time. These similarities seem more pronounced during periods of intense media attention. Support was also found for the notion that the print media lead the television networks rather than the reverse. More specific analyses are conducted in the next chapter, viewing this leadership process from day to day and from week to week. This study was confined to examining manifest media content, which can only imply the processes of leadership suggested above. More in-depth studies of these actual processes and the newsworkers involved would help shed more light on the role of intermedia influence in the media convergence process. Given the value traditionally attached to diversity in American society, it is important to fully understand such processes which directly affect the extent of that diversity.

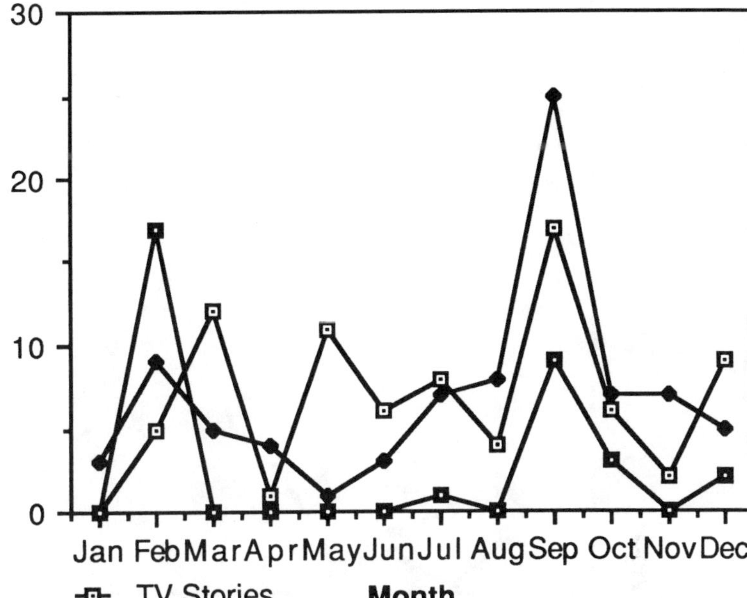

FIG. 5.5   1985 cross-media cocaine issue coverage.

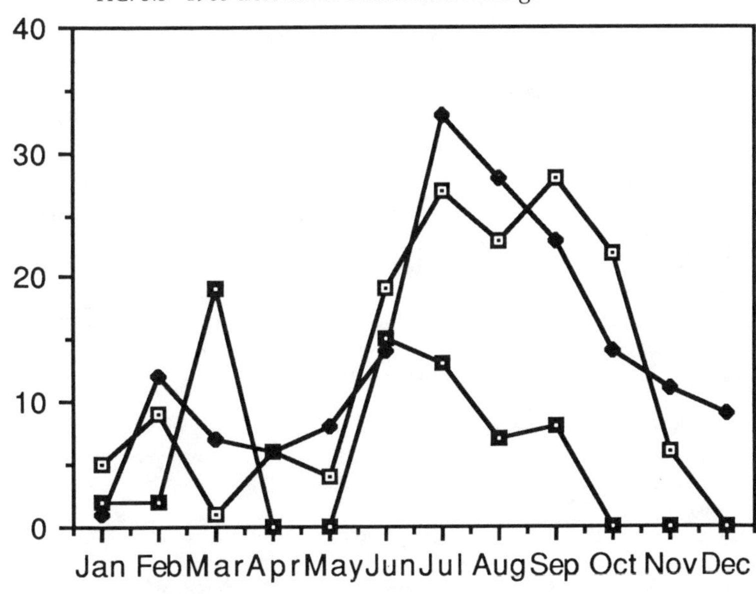

FIG. 5.6   1986 cross-media cocaine issue coverage.

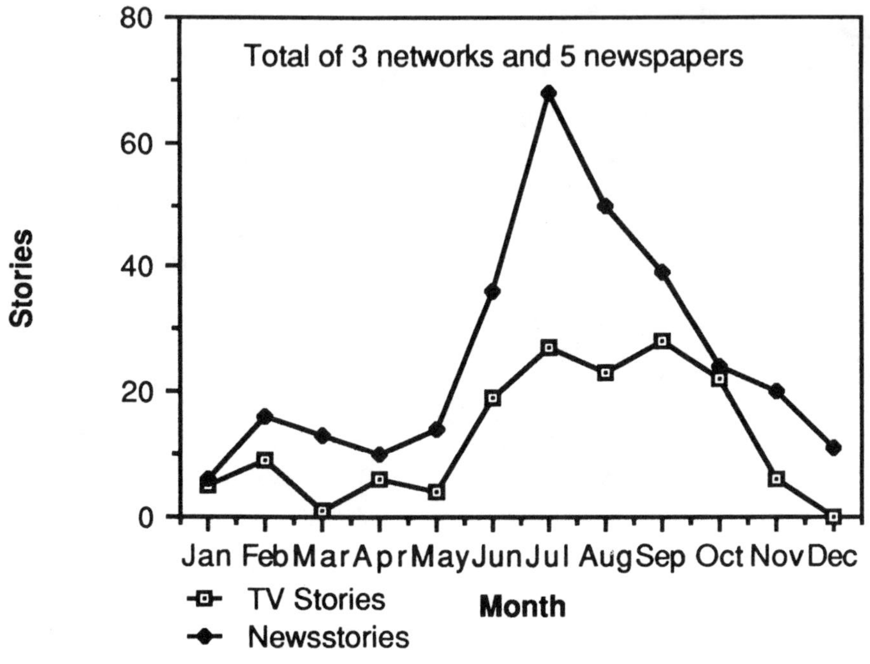

FIG. 5.7.   1986 cross-media cocaine issue coverage.

REFERENCES

Altheide, D.L. (1982). Three-in-one news: Network coverage of Iran. *Journalism Quarterly,*
59, 482–486.
Atwater, T., Fico, F., & Pizante, G. (1987). Reporting on the state legislature: A case of
inter-media agenda setting. *Newspaper Research Journal, 8,* 52–61.
Bigman, S.K. (1984). Rivals in conformity: A study of two competing dailies. *Journalism*
Quarterly, 25, 127–131.
Breed, W. (1980). Dissertations on sociology: The newspaperman, news and society.
New York: Arno Press.
Buckalew, J. K. (1969). News elements and selection by television news editors. *Journal of*
Broadcasting, 14, 47–54.
Capo, J.A. (1983). Network Watergate coverage patterns in late 1972 and early 1973.
Journalism Quarterly, 60, 595–602.
Diamond, E. (1987, February 7). Is TV news hyping America's cocaine problem? *TV*
Guide, pp. 4–10.
Dominick, J.R. (1981). Business coverage in network newscasts. *Journalism Quarterly, 58,*
179–185.
Donohue, T. R., & Glasser, T. L. (1978). Homogeneity in coverage of Connecticut
newspapers. *Journalism Quarterly, 55,* 592–596.
Foote, J., & Steele, M. E. (1986). Degree of conformity in lead stories in early evening
network TV newscasts. *Journalism Quarterly, 63,* 19–23.
Fowler, J. S., & Showalter, S. W. (1974). Evening network news selection. A confirma-
tion of news judgment. *Journalism Quarterly, 51,* 712–715.
Gans, H. (1979). *Deciding what's news.* New York: Random House.

Graber, D. (1971). Press coverage patterns of campaign news: The 1968 presidential race. Journalism Quarterly, 48, 502–512.

Hatch, R. (1987). Drugs, politics, and disinformation. *Covert Action Information Bulletin, 28,* 23–27.

Hester, A. (1978). Five years of foreign news in U.S. television evening newscasts. *Gazette, 24,* 88–95.

Kerr, P. (1986, November 17). Anatomy of an issue: Drugs, the evidence, the reaction. *The New York Times,* p. 1.

Lemert, J. B. (1974). Content duplication by the networks in competing evening newscasts. *Journalism Quarterly, 51,* 238–244.

Massing, M. (1984). The network newscasts: Still hot off the presses. *Channels, 47,* 47–52.

McCombs, M., & Shaw, D. (1972). The agenda setting function of the mass media. *Public Opinion Quarterly, 36,* 176–184.

Meeske, M. D., & Javaheri, M. H. (1982). Network television coverage of the Iranian hostage crisis. *Journalism Quarterly, 59,* 641–645.

Miller, S. H. (1978). Reporters and congressmen: Living in symbiosis. *Journalism Monographs, 53,*

Parenti, M. (1986). Inventing reality: The politics of the mass media. New York: St. Martin's Press.

Prichard, P. (1987, October). The McPapering of America: An insider's candid account. *Washington Journalism Review,* pp. 32–37.

Riffe, D., & Shaw, E.F. (1982). Conflict and consonance. Coverage of third world in two U.S. papers. *Journalism Quarterly, 59,* 484–488.

Riffe, D., Ellis, B., Rogers, M.K., Van Ommeren, R.L., & Woodman, K. A. (1986). Gatekeeping and the network news mix. *Journalism Quarterly, 63,* 315–321.

Sigal, L.V. (1973). *Reporters and officials: The organization and politics of newsmaking.* Lexington, MA: D.C. Heath.

Stempel, G. H., & Windhauser, J. W. (1984). The prestige press revisited: Coverage of the 1980 presidential campaign. *Journalism Quarterly, 61,* 49–55.

Weaver, J. B., Porter, C. J., & Evans, M. E. (1984). Patterns of foreign news coverage on U.S. network TV: A 10-year analysis. *Journalism Quarterly, 61,* 356–363.

Weaver, D., & Wilhoit, G. C. (1986). *The American journalist.* Bloomington, IN: Indiana University Press.

A Closer Look at Intermedia Influences on Agenda Setting: The Cocaine Issue of 1986

Lucig H. Danielian
Stephen D. Reese
University of Texas

The agenda-setting process has been described as a full circle, "beginning with the impact of the social system on media institutions, and then, on their members, particularly reporters and editors. These media operatives make decisions which, the evidence shows, have impact on the cognitions of the media audience member" (Becker, McCombs, & McLeod, 1975). Much of the agenda-setting model has been mapped out and strong evidence has been gathered to support the impact of the mass media agenda on that of the audience, but there has been little research on how the mass media agenda is formed in their review of the agenda setting research of the last 25 years. Rogers and Dearing (1988) identify four factors that influence news media agendas: (a) the structure of society, (b) real world indicators, (c) spectacular news events, and (d) gatekeepers and influential media. This fourth factor is examined in this chapter—the extent to which the media influence each other. We refer to it as *intermedia agenda setting.*

As we explained in the preceding chapter, we selected a single issue for our focus—the cocaine issue of 1985 and 1986. We see the drug issue in 1985 and 1986 as having more to do with intermedia agenda setting than with the structure of society, real-world indicators, or even spectacular news events, although of course these factors play some role in most stories. Our reasoning is based on the fact that actual drug use did not rise dramatically in 1985 and 1986, as did mass media coverage of cocaine. On the contrary, cocaine use in particular had been leveling off since the late 1970s, and, although a new drug, crack, was a problem in certain urban areas, there was no evidence of a real drug "epidemic" (Baker, 1986;

Kerr, 1986). Therefore, this issue provides a good opportunity for looking at ways in which the news media themselves may have contributed to such a concentrated amount of cocaine coverage in such a short period of time.

By tracing coverage of one issue over time, we hope to better isolate the leading and following tendencies of the news media rather than simple cross-media similarities. In chapter 5, we examined patterns of coverage across the major print and broadcast news organizations in order to determine the extent of media convergence. We found substantial intermedia similarities in the amount of coverage given the cocaine issue during the years 1985 and 1986 by the major national news media.

The New York Times surpassed the other newspapers we studied (including *The Wall Street Journal, The Washington Post,* and *The Los Angeles Times*) in its amount of coverage of the cocaine story during 1985 and the first half of 1986. The other papers appeared to fall in line by the summer of 1986, giving the issue similar high attention. We also found indications that the print media, especially *The New York Times*, set the agenda for the network newscasts coverage of cocaine. Thus, a general intermedia agenda setting influence was noted from *The New York Times* to the other media.

This chapter extends our intermedia analysis by examining the same news media on a week-to-week rather than month-to-month basis. In addition to examining the amount of cocaine coverage, we also look at the actual story content of the four newspapers for selected peak weeks and examine their themes and sources in order to better trace intermedia influence processes taking place on a daily basis in the daily press.

COMPARING MEDIA COVERAGE
FROM WEEK TO WEEK

In the previous chapter we showed that the media followed each other from month-to-month in coverage of the cocaine issue. These similarities in attention suggest that the media influence each other's agenda from month to month. We would expect to find the same agenda similarities from week to week and from day to day.

Our week-to-week analysis focuses on a period extending from April through December of 1986. As seen in Fig. 5.3 and 5.4 in the preceding chapter, this period features a normal-like curve of rising and falling coverage and is the peak period of coverage over the 2 years of our study. The national news media analyzed in this chapter include three newspapers, three television newscasts, and two news magazines: *The New York Times; The Washington Post; The LostAngeles Times; The Wall Street Journal;* the nightly network newscasts of ABC, CBS, and NBC; and *Time* and *Newsweek*.[1]

As in the study discussed in the previous chapter, the DIALOG information service was used to electronically access newspaper and magazine databases for cocaine stories.[2] Bibliographic information and a short story summary were obtained for each story. A similar search strategy was used to find the network news stories. The Vanderbilt University Television News Index and Abstract was searched for stories indexed under "cocaine," and these stories were coded for date and length in seconds. The searches resulted in 465 newspaper stories, 231 network news stories, and 44 newsmagazine stories.

Each story was coded with high intercoder agreement ($cr = .90$) into 1 of 10 story catagories: (a) *deaths* of prominent people and the events surrounding them; (b) specific *crime* crimes involving cocaine, trials, arrests, and so on; (c) *the antidrug movement* in schools and communities and by national figures aimed at discouraging the use of cocaine; (d) general reports on the *use and abuse* of cocaine and on its various medical and social implications; (e) four categories dealing with *policy responses* by the *national, state and local, international,* and *private sectors*; (f) problems encountered by *foreign* countries in combating drugs (without reference to direct U.S. involvement); and (g) extensive reports on the *general drug crisis.*

Correlating the Weekly Amount of Coverage

During the 40-week study period, from March 30 through December 31, 1986, 406 stories were found to deal with cocaine. A week of coverage is defined as beginning on Sunday and ending with Saturday.

The New York Times carried 139 cocaine stories during these 40 weeks, followed by *The Washington Post* with 60, *The Los Angeles Times* with 38, and *The Wall Street Journal* with 13 stories – 260 newspaper stories in all. The three nightly television network newscasts covered the cocaine issue with 129 stories – ABC ran 34 stories, CBS 49, and NBC 46. *Time* and *Newsweek* magazines ran 8 and 9 stories, respectively.

Table 6.1 shows the coverage broken down by category and type of medium. The distribution is similar to the entire 1985/1986 period (see Table 5.3, this volume), with "crime" and "use and abuse" stories getting the most prominent coverage. When the four subcategories are combined, we can see that the "policy response" category is also given heavy

---

[1]We dropped the *Christian Science Monitor* from this in-depth study because its contribution was found to be insignificant in our overall look at agenda setting over the 2-year period of our original study (see chapter 5).

[2]We limited our search to the term *cocaine* in order to narrow the scope of the search into a manageable, yet comparable, sample of stories across media.

TABLE 6.1
Nature of Cocaine Stories During 1986 Study Period. Frequency of Story Types
by Combined Media–Newspapers, News Magazines, and Television Networks

| | *Medium* | | |
Type of Story	*Newspapers*	*News Magazines*	*Networks*
Deaths	13%	18%	13%
Crime	29	6	25
Antidrug movement	7	6	4
Use and abuse	25	18	29
Policy Response			
National	3	6	10
State/local	5	0	3
International	10	24	8
Private sector	0	0	4
Foreign	6	12	4
General crisis	2	12	0
Total	100%	100%	100%
N	(260)	(17)	(129)

play, with international and national policies being the most prominent
topics.

Pearson correlation coefficients between the number of cocaine stories
covered by each medium during each week demonstrate the extent to
which the major news media's attention to cocaine rose and fell simultaneously during the 40-week period (see Table 6.2). The unit of analysis is
the week ($n = 40$) with summed coverage measures (newspaper column
inches, television seconds, news magazine pages) for each medium for
each week.

We expected some similarities in coverage across media, if only due to
their covering the same dramatic or specific events. For example, many of
the stories in our census dealt with the tragic deaths of famous people like
John Belushi, Len Bias, and Don Rogers and with routine crime news
such as arrests, seizures, and trials. And indeed we do see many statistically significant correlation coefficients in the bottom half of Fig. 6.2,
showing that overall media coverage of cocaine did rise and fall in concert
at least part of the time.

We suspected, however, that media coverage of cocaine did not change
only in response to newsworthy events such as deaths and crimes.
Therefore, we deleted these "event-driven" categories and recalculated the
correlation coefficients to determine if the observed relationships in
coverage among the media were due simply to the media covering the
same spectacular news events. The correlation coefficients representing
similarities in the media's more issue-oriented coverage (all categories

TABLE 6.2
Correlations Between Major Media in Amount of Coverage Given Cocaine
Stories in Newspaper Column Inches, Television Seconds, News Magazine
Pages

	Newspapers				TV Networks			News Magazines	
	NYT	*WSJ*	*Post*	*LAT*	*ABC*	*CBS*	*NBC*	*Time*	*Nwsk*
NYT	–	.10	.46***	.45**	.31*	.18	.35*	.18	.08
WSJ	.29*	–	.00	.06	−.12	−.13	−.02	−.09	−.02
Post	.44**	−.11	–	.48***	.36*	.13	.44**	.12	.03
LAT	.38**	−.01	.26[a]	–	.33*	.46**	.61***	−.15	−.11
ABC	.24	−.16	.54***	.23	–	.28*	.36*	.58***	−.07
CBS	.18	−.17	.20	.37[b]	.32*	–	.48***	−.15	−.12
NBC	.23	.05	.43[b]	.47[b]	.47***	.48***	–	−.09	.12
Time	.10	−.14	.36*	−.08	.56***	−.08	.11	–	.29*
Nwsk	.08	−.05	.05	.12	.10	−.08	−.08	.21	–

*$p < .05$
**$p < .01$
***$p < .001$

Note: The bottom triangle contains correlations between coverage measures based on all cocaine stories. The top triangle of correlations is based on measures excluding "crime" and "prominent deaths" stories.

except those representing crime and prominent deaths) appear in the top triangle of Table 6.2.

We can address several important questions with these results. How strong were intramedium similarities in the amount of cocaine coverage, that is, convergence among the members of one medium (e.g., newspapers)? Did the major newspapers devote similar amounts of coverage to cocaine at similar times, implying a cross-media agenda-setting process? Or did one newspaper appear to be more consistently correlated with all the others, implying a leadership role? How strong were intermedia similarities, or convergence, among the various media? And, finally, do these relationships differ for overall and issue-oriented coverage?

Of the four newspapers examined, *The Wall Street Journal*'s cocaine coverage was the least associated with that of the other newspapers. Although both the *Journal* and *The New York Times* are distributed nationally to an elite audience, the *Journal*'s focus on business news may have lessened the newsworthiness of cocaine-related stories. *The New York Times'* cocaine coverage, however, was significantly correlated with each of the other newspapers' coverage of all cocaine stories, thus supporting the general view of *The New York Times* as a leader among the newspapers.

Did the television news networks follow each other closely in the timing and amount of coverage given to cocaine? The correlation coefficients are of roughly the same magnitude as those among the newspapers. All three correlation coefficients among the television networks are statistically significant in both sets of correlations—those representing all story types and those for just issue-oriented stories.[3]

Finally, *Time* and *Newsweek*'s cocaine coverages were significantly associated for the "issue"-oriented correlations, those stories excluding the crime and death categories. The two news magazines' cocaine coverages were not significantly correlated with each other when all stories were included in the analysis.[4]

We also looked at whether cocaine coverage was similar across the media and found substantial relationships for "intermedia" agenda setting. Network television coverage of cocaine was generally related to newspaper coverage, except for *The Wall Street Journal,* whose cocaine coverage was not significantly correlated with that of any network. CBS appears to be the most individualistic of the networks; its coverage was associated with only that of *The Los Angeles Times*. In fact, of the four newspapers, only *The Los Angeles Times'* cocaine coverage was significantly correlated with that of all three television networks.

It is interesting to note that there are stronger and more significant relationships among the newspapers and the television networks when crime and death news is excluded (statistically significant correlations range from .31 to .61). Looking at groups of coefficients in Table 5.2, 7 of the 12 newspaper/television correlations for stories excluding crime and prominent deaths reached significance. Only four of the newspaper/ television correlations for all stories (lower triangle) were significant.

As for the news magazines, they showed almost no significant correlations with either the networks or newspapers (except for between *Time* and the *Post* for all stories). The strong association between *Time* and ABC news may have been due to a one-time coincidence between a cover story issue and an ABC series that same week. In the future, we will look at news-gathering structures that link the mainstream media. These include shared wire services, joint polling activities, syndicated satellite networks, and so forth. These intermedia structures may help explain similarities in content.

Overall, media follow others of the same type more closely than they do other media types. Excluding *The Wall Street Journal,* the newspapers are all significantly interrelated, as are the three networks. Newspapers are

---

[3]These correlations are not so high, though, as to justify calling the networks, as does Altheide (1982), a "national news service" featuring indistinguishable content.

[4]It is interesting to note that both magazines ran cocaine stories before the study period, running simultaneous covers in February on the cocaine wars in South America. *Newsweek* ran a cover on crack in the middle of March and a later cover story on crack in June which fell within the 40-week census period.

less consistently related to the networks, although there are substantial correlations. Newspapers show more significant relationships with networks for those more general drug issue stories, excluding crimes and prominent deaths. Fewer significant relationships are found between newspapers and networks when all story types are included. For example, Table 6.2 shows that for all stories, *The New York Times* is unrelated to the networks. This may be due to the fact that the *Times* covered many local drug stories, such as criminal activities, that were not suitable for the national evening news broadcasts. As mentioned, the news magazines show few relationships with the other media. These outlets may have a significant intermedia influence role, but it may not be apparent in week-to-week variations.

Week-to-Week Trends in Cocaine Coverage

So far in this analysis, we have looked at relationships among the media's coverage of cocaine. High correlation coefficients show that organizations transmitted similar weekly amounts of cocaine coverage, either large or small, during the 40-week period of our analysis. However, these correlation coefficients do not take into account how the coverage of cocaine by one medium in a preceding week or weeks may lead to greater attention by other media in following weeks. In order to identify these leading and following tendencies, we graphed newspaper and television cocaine coverage for the entire 40-week period.[5] These charts show coverage for only the "issue"-oriented stories. Crime and death, the more "event-driven" categories have been excluded from this analysis. The 40-week study period is divided into four sets of graphs for easier viewing, each made up of a 10-week period.

One example of leadership influence occurred during the first 10 weeks of the study period (see Fig. 6.1). *The Washington Post* ran four related articles on cocaine on May 14, 1986 (during week 7 of our analysis). And on the following Sunday, May 18, 1986 (week 8), *The New York Times* ran a major story on cocaine (as did two other New York city newspapers). Peter Kerr (1986) marked this point as one of the media milestones in "discovering" the cocaine issue.

In addition to looking at leadership among the newspapers, we can also see that the newspapers apparently also provided leadership for the

---

[5]We chose this descriptive route over more statistical methods, such as cross-lagged correlations, because such methods require more theoretical assumptions than we are prepared to make now. For example, a consistent time lag among the media types would have to be present to produce such relationships. However, we hope this initial descriptive study will help to build toward more systematic theoretical and methodological methods.

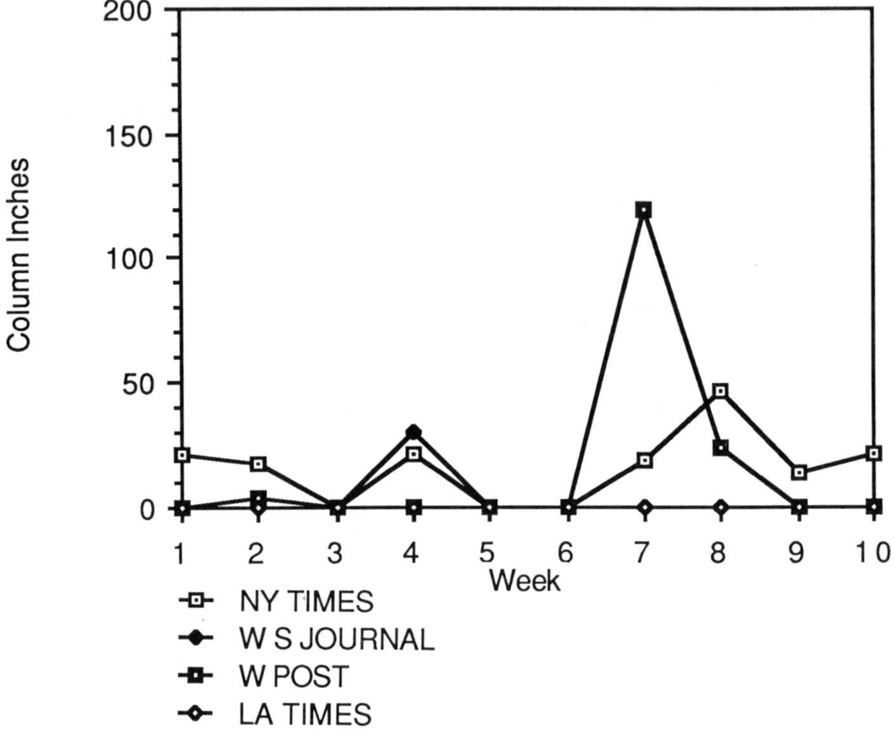

FIG. 6.1.   Newspaper coverage excluding crime and death weeks 1–10 (March 30 through June 7).

television networks (see Fig. 6.2). NBC followed *The New York Times'* lead with cocaine coverage later in the week, while ABC and CBS aired cocaine stories during the following week (week 9 in Fig. 6.2, May 25–31, 1986).

Figures 6.3 and 6.4 show the rise and fall in cocaine coverage for both newspapers and the television networks during our second 10-week period. *The New York Times* generally ran more cocaine coverage than did the other newspapers at each point in time, although changes over time in the amounts of the four newspapers' cocaine coverage were similar. During the same time period, the television networks followed the peaks of attention shown by the newspapers, although they did not stay with the story quite as long.

Although news magazine coverage is not shown, it is worth noting that *Time* did a multipage cocaine story during week 12 (June 15–21, 1986); both news magazines carried major cocaine stories during week 18 (July 27 to August 2). These news magazine stories preceded increases in

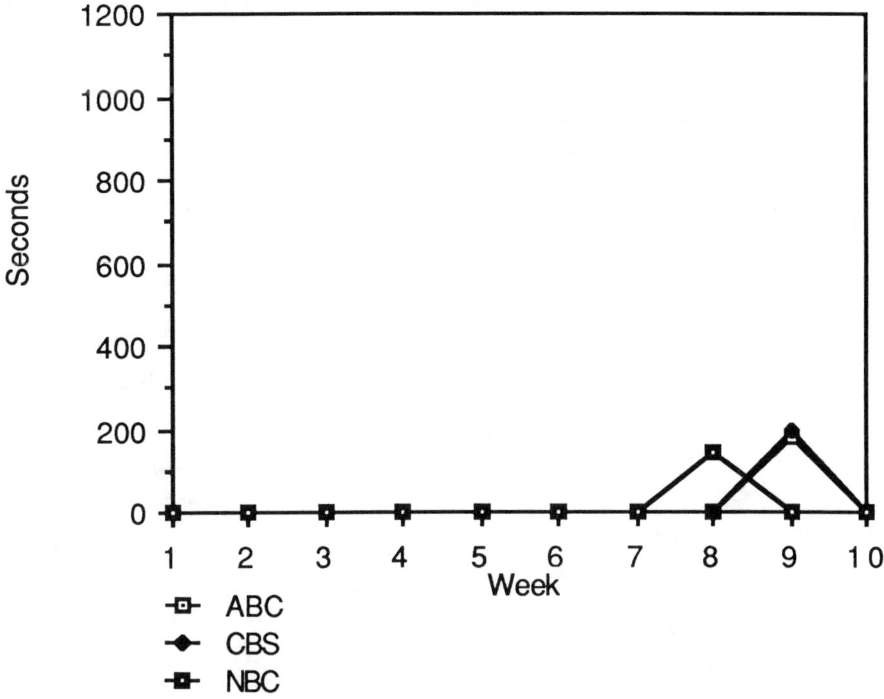

FIG. 6.2. Television coverage excluding crime and death weeks 1–10 (March 30 through June 7).

coverage by the newspaper and television networks during the following week, indicating some leadership by the news magazines.

In the third 10-week period, still other media influences on cocaine coverage are suggested (see Fig. 6.5 and 6.6). *The New York Times* shows a spike in coverage in week 24 (September 7–13, 1986), followed the next week by a major *Time* magazine cocaine story and by coverage in the *Washington Post*. ABC followed with almost 20 minutes worth of cocaine news that same week. *The Los Angeles Times* and the other networks increased their coverage during the next week. An increase in coverage by *The New York Times* in week 27 (September 28 through October 4) was followed in turn by an increase during the next week in coverage by the CBS and NBC nightly newscasts. (ABC already had a great deal of coverage by this time.)

This reciprocal, back-and-forth attention cycle suggests that the issue was kept in the news by first one medium and then another dealing with it in turn, each perhaps reinforced by the preceding week's coverage and indicating a sort of "epidemic" of media interest in the cocaine issue.

Newspaper and television coverage for the final 10-week period of

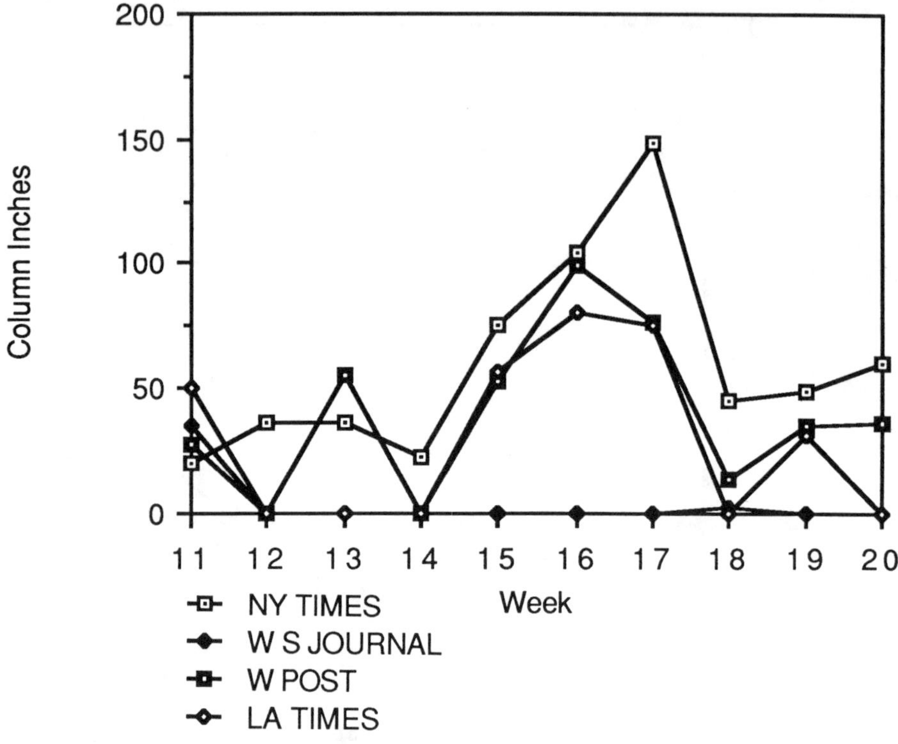

FIG. 6.3. Newspaper coverage excluding crime and death weeks 11–20 (June 9 through August 16).

1986 are shown in Fig. 6.7 and 6.8 (October 26 through December 31, 1986). *The New York Times* "carried" the issue for the media during this period, and its coverage spiked sharply in week 34 (November 16–22). The news magazines were the first to drop the drug story (week 25), followed by the television networks (week 34, coinciding with the big spike in the *Times*), and finally by the newspapers (week 38).

These results show that *The New York Times* did lead cocaine coverage for the other media in some instances and that it covered the story the longest and the most consistently. However, the news magazines and other influential dailies also played a part in keeping the issue before the public. There were some weeks where media coverage seemed to converge, whereas in others the media appeared to alternate covering cocaine from week to week, first one medium and then another giving the issue heavy play, until all joined in.

These graphs help demonstrate that cocaine coverage in the mass media did not monolithicly rise and fall during 1986, with the media marching in lockstep close behind *The New York Times*. Rather, the trends

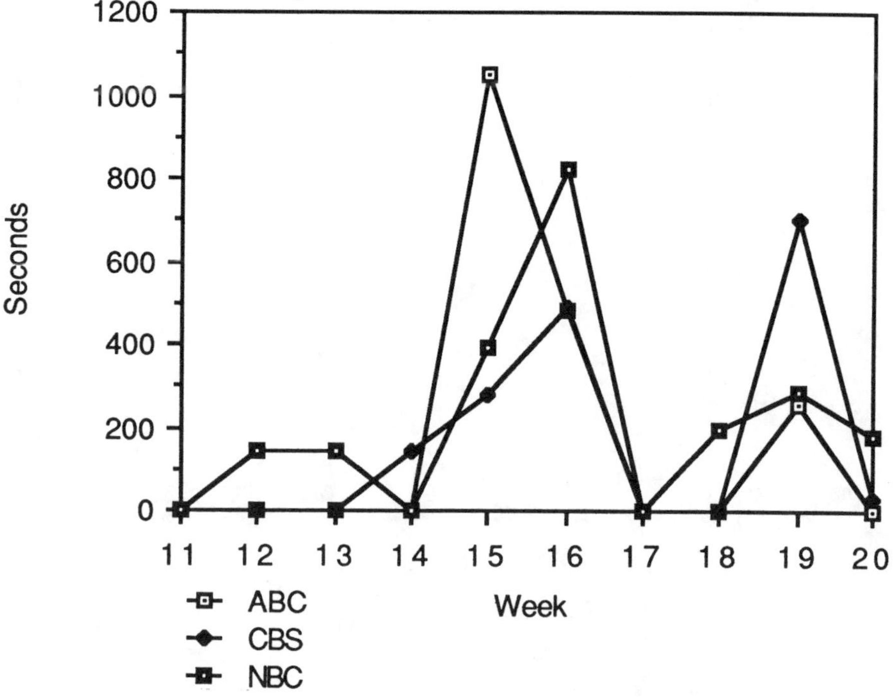

FIG. 6.4.   Telelvision coverage excluding crime and death weeks 11–20 (June 8 through August 16).

of increasing and decreasing attention to the drug issue during the last two-thirds of 1986 can be seen as many separate changes in the separate media's attention to cocaine.

The intermedia agenda setting process is more like a square dance than a forced march – the patterns and partners continually change as both external events and the media "dancers" themselves call the steps.

NEWS SOURCES AND THEMES: NEWSPAPER INTERMEDIA AGENDA SETTING

Studying the amount of coverage the media transmit about cocaine over time tells only a part of the tale. In this part of the chapter, we use a qualitative approach to dissect the processes taking place in intermedia agenda setting. We examine the extent to which prominent sources may create similarities in media coverage. In general, the more national the story, and in particular the more national the sources, the more we expect convergence on a story. We use the term *convergence* to describe a process

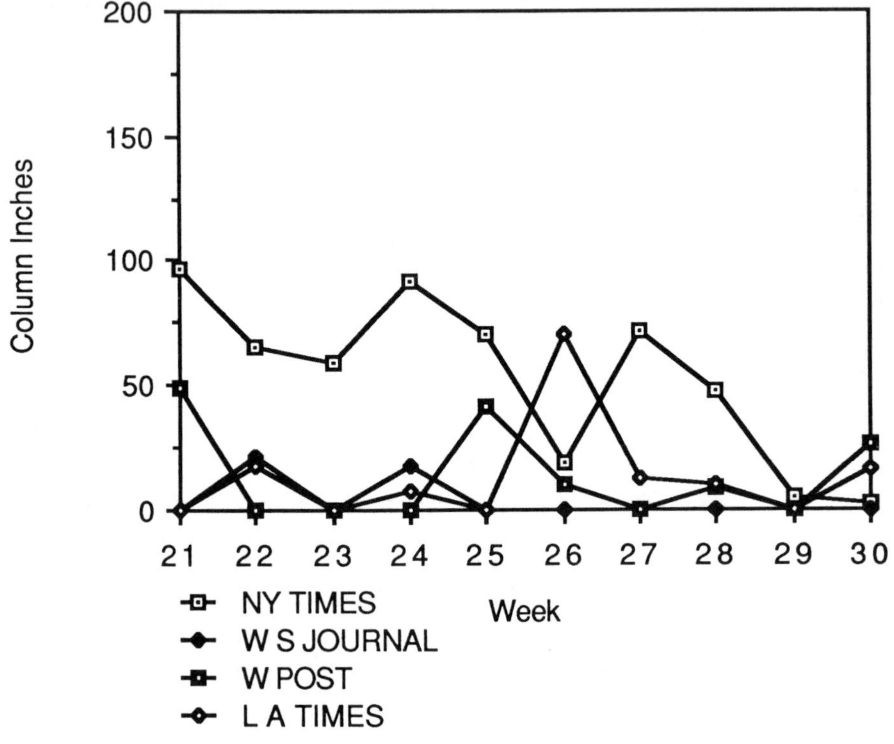

FIG. 6.5. Newspaper coverage excluding crime and death weeks 21–30 (August 17 through October 25).

in which the media discover issues and respond to each other in a cycle of peaking coverage. For example, we expect more homogeneous coverage when the story comes from the nation's capital, Washington DC.

Gans (1979) suggested that sources are covered most when they have: (a) incentives, (b) power, (c) the ability to supply suitable information, and (d) geographic and social proximity to journalists. All four conditions are satisfied by administration sources based in the District of Columbia, whom Gans referred to as "national leaders." Also lending support to Gans' summation is Sigal's (1973) analysis of the content of *The New York Times* and *The Washington Post*. Sigal found that 74% of the sources of information for all news stories were made up of U.S. officials and agencies and of foreign or international officials and agencies.

To more closely examine the influence processes that are suggested in the quantitative analyses, all issue-oriented cocaine stories in the four newspapers (*The New York Times, The Washington Post, The Los Angeles Times, and The Wall Street Journal*) during the 40-week study period were located

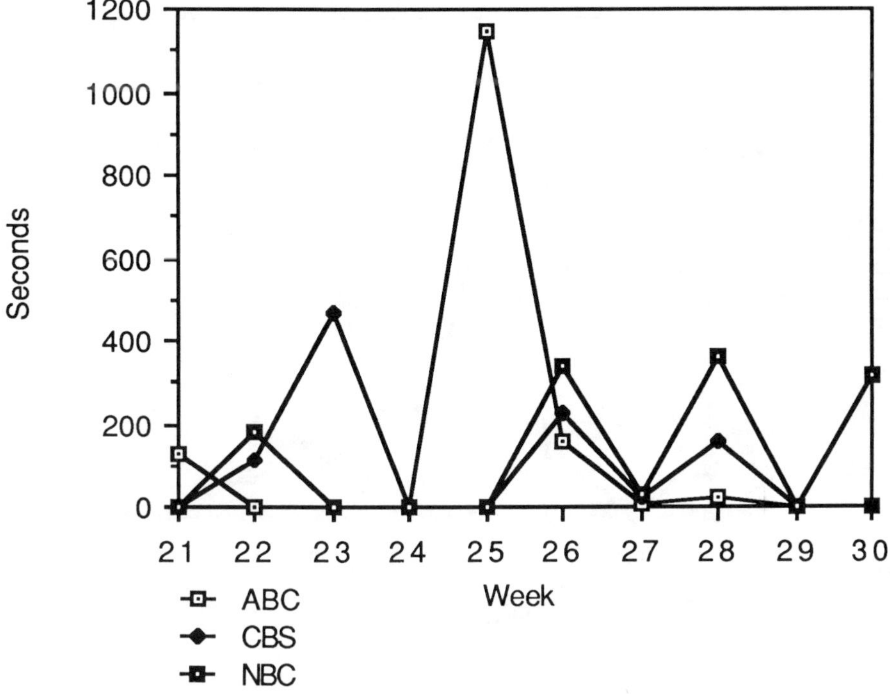

FIG. 6.6. Television coverage excluding crime and death weeks 21–30 (August 17 through October 25).

on microfilm and photocopied. We then culled through this 40-week supply of articles. We sought to identify those weeks during which all four newspapers had cocaine stories, under the assumption that such coverage is necessary before intermedia processes can be seen on a daily basis. Because only one such week was found (week 11 – June 8–14) due to *The Wall Street Journal*'s not covering the cocaine story heavily, those weeks in which three of the four newspapers carried stories were also identified. Ten such weeks were located, and from these the weeks exhibiting the most total newspaper coverage were chosen for a textual analysis. This peak period, easily seen in Fig. 6.3, is made up of weeks 15, 16, and 17 (July 6–26, 1986). The stories in this 3-week period were analyzed for sources used and for the general themes of the news stories.

Week 11, the one week in which all four newspapers covered cocaine stories, is by no means a "peak" period (see Fig. 6.3), but it provides some interesting insights. On June 8, 1986, *The New York Times* ran a front-page story, "Crack Addition Spreads Among the Middle Class," with the focus on New York City. It was followed on June 10 by two stories with a business peg in *The Wall Street Journal*, one a two-paragraph front-page

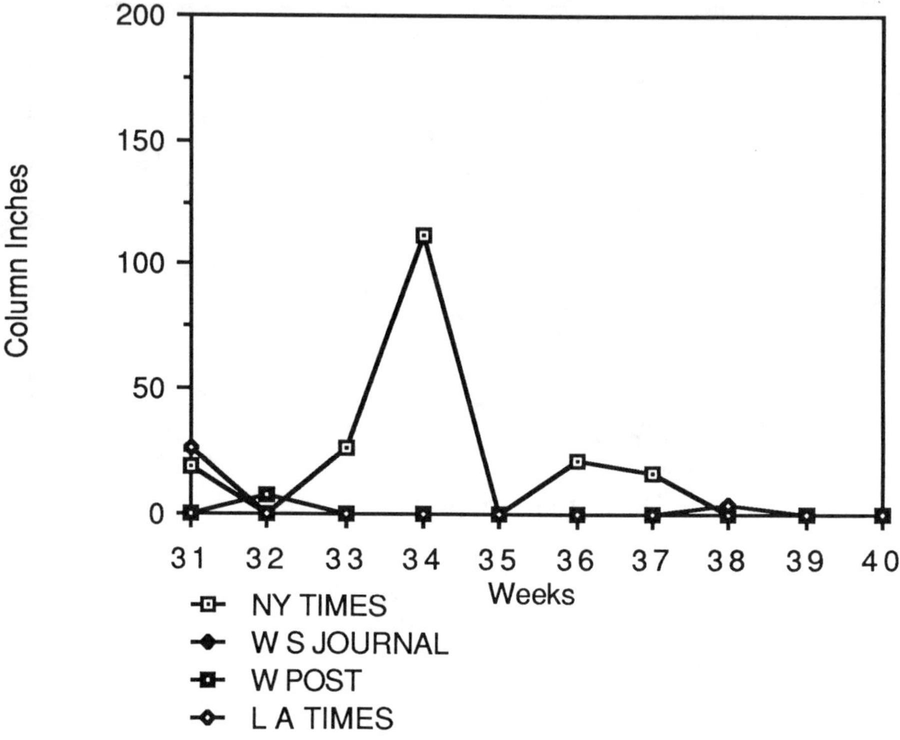

FIG. 6.7. Newspaper coverage excluding crime and death weeks 31–40) (October 26 through December 31).

story, "Crack Addiction – Executives Are Tougher to Treat than Blue Collar Workers," and the other an opinion column, "Lessons of the First Cocaine Epidemic." *The Los Angeles Times* came in next with a California story "Crank [sic] Labs Cooking Up More of Poor Man's Cocaine." (They referred to the new drug as "crank" instead of "crack.") On June 13, *The Washington Post* closed the week's coverage with a New York datelined story, "Crack Making Violent Presence Felt in New York." The three east coast papers all used a national cocaine hotline report as a source, but they put their own spins on the story. Nevertheless, *The New York Times* was definitely in the lead chronologically.

The New York Times, *The Washington Post*, and *The Los Angeles Times* covered the story during the 3-week "peak" period from week 15 through week 17. This period provides an interesting look at some patterns among the newspapers.

Ten stories were found in week 15–4 in *The New York Times*, 3 in *The Washington Post*, and 3 in *The Los Angeles Times*. All three newspapers covered a July 11 story based on a National Institute on Drug Abuse report

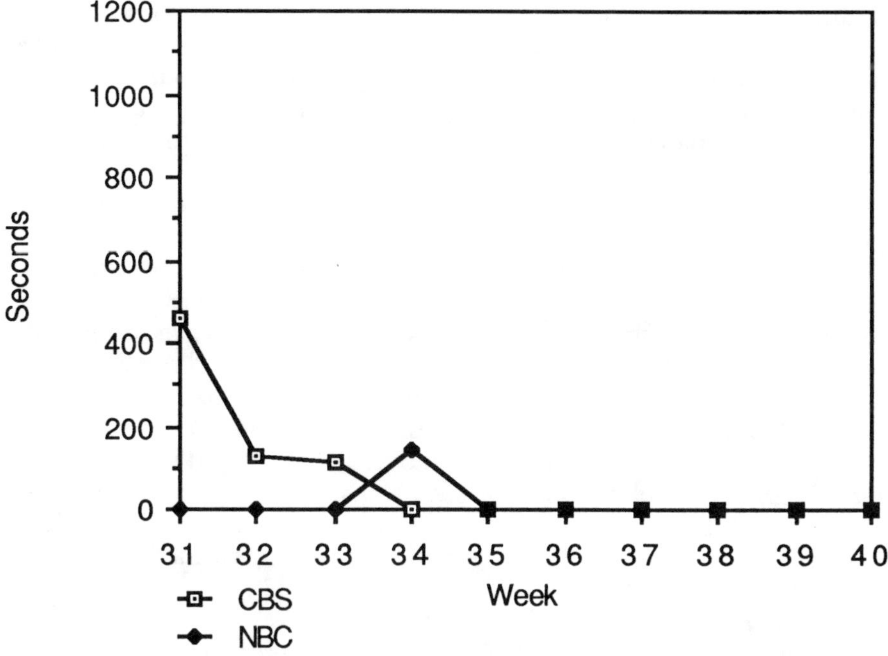

FIG. 6.8.   Television coverage excluding crime and death weeks 31–40 (October 26 through December 31).

with front-page coverage and a DC dateline. A July 8 story, based on a survey funded by the National Institute on Drug Abuse, made it into both *The New York Times* and *The Washington Post*, again with DC datelines.

The Los Angeles Times (July 6) and *The Washington Post* (July 9) both covered a UPI story out of Boston on cocaine and premature labor. But, *The Los Angeles Times* actually led the week's coverage with an extensive front-page science report, "Medications Found to Block Cocaine's Effects." *The New York Times* also did a story with a local peg that ran on page 1 of its July 11 metropolitan section on the need for more federal action against cocaine, as well as a long sports section story the same day by Tony Eliot of the New Orleans Saints, "How Cocaine Took Control of My Life."

Although *The New York Times* led in the number of cocaine stories during this week, the national stories coming out of Washington DC seem to create the most convergence among the newspapers, especially as we look at the process from week to week. It is important to note that the preceding week had minimal coverage, none for *The Washington Post* or *The Los Angeles Times* and only two shorter stories in *The New York Times*.

Fifteen stories on cocaine made up week 16 coverage—6 for *The New York Times*, 4 for *The Washington Post*, and 5 for *The Los Angeles Times*.

Thirteen of these stories dealt with the U.S.-assisted raid on Bolivian cocaine operations (*The New York Times* and *The Washington Post* at 4 stories and *The Los Angeles Times* at 5). Actually, it is little wonder that such convergence existed when the story finally broke on Tuesday, July 16. All three newspapers sat on the story in order to protect the operation.[6] They broke the story only when newspapers in Santa Cruz, Bolivia, published alarmed reports about the landing of a huge U.S. transport plane bearing helicopters.

All three U.S. newspapers used the same unnamed administration and Bolivian officials as sources. Sidebar stories on July 16 focused on the use of the military in the operation, with *The New York Times* using both administration officials, citizen rights groups (ACLU and the Center for Constitutional Rights), and other experts such as law professors as sources. *The Washington Post* sidebar concentrated on Vice President Bush's successful lobbying for military action over Pentagon and Defense Secretary Weinberger's objections. *The Los Angeles Times* featured a front-page story on July 17, "U.S. May Aid Anti-Cocaine Assaults in Peru, Columbia," (clearly not wanting to be left behind again) with a focus on the Bush/Weinberger debate.

All three newspapers also covered a more "issue"-oriented Bolivian story on July 18 with La Paz, Bolivia, datelines focusing on Fernando Barthelemy, Bolivia's Minister of the Interior. *The New York Times, The Washington Post,* and *The Los Angeles Times* headlines are similar and read, respectively, "Bolivia Says Its Drive in Cocaine Will Go On Until Tade is Ended," "Bolivia Vows to End Drug Traffic," and "Bolivia Vows to 'Root Out' Cocaine Producers." The July 16 and 18 stories were written by the same foreign reporters for each of the newspapers. (Joel Brinkley for *The New York Times,* Bradley Graham for *The Washington Post,* and Juan de Onis for *The Los Angeles Times* wrote nearly all of the Bolivian stories during weeks 16 and 17.) The same writers also got stories printed on July 19 in both *The New York Times* and *The Washington Post* on a successful raid on a Bolivian cocaine factory. The source for these stories was Bolivia's Minister of Information, Herman Antelo.

The Los Angeles Times was the only newspaper to cover Defense Secretary Weinberger's San Diego speech to the local Chamber of Commerce in which he "decried" the Bolivian leaks. (In this article, *The Los Angeles Times* noted that it had held the Bolivian story the longest. In an earlier

---

[6]Both *The Los Angeles Times* and *The Washington Post* had verified the story with administration officials at least a week in advance, whereas *The New York Times* claims not to have had the story until Monday, July 15, 1986 (*The New York Times,* 1986). *The Los Angeles Times* actually held the story until July 17 and then printed it on page 14.

title it had inaccurately claimed it broke the story along with the others in an earlier article.)

The coverage during week 16 helps clarify the intermedia convergence patterns among newspapers: When a story broke with national leaders as the source of information, convergence followed among the newspapers on the same day.

Our last week of analysis also demonstrates that nationally based stories lead to the greatest amount of convergence on story themes and sources. Week 17 included 14 cocaine stories, and once again the majority of the stories focused on the foreign situation. Five of the 7 *New York Times* stories were about Bolivia, while 2 of the 3 *Washington Post* stories and 3 of the 4 *Los Angeles Times* stories focused on the Bolivian situation.

During this last week of the peak in cocaine coverage, the story themes and sources began to vary somewhat. Both *The New York Times* and *The Los Angeles Times* covered the cocaine issue, but with different pegs. On July 20, 1986, *The New York Times* published two and *The Los Angeles Times* published one Bolivian cocaine story. One of *The New York Times* stories, "Bolivians Deny They Asked U.S. to Send Troops to Help in Raids," had a La Paz dateline and used White House and Bolivian officials as sources. *The Los Angeles Times* used various nonleadership sources (mostly peasant cooperatives) for its La Paz datelined story, "Bolivia Unions, Leftists Decry U.S. Role in Drug Raids."

The Los Angeles Times led with a July 22 story out of La Paz based on a press conference with Minister of Information Antelo headlined, "Bolivia Claims Victory Over Cocaine." The next day, both *The New York Times* and *The Washington Post* got on the bandwagon with their own stories based on a news conference with Interior Minister Barthelemy and U.S. officials on the success of the Bolivian operations.

Interviews with Bolivian President Paz and Planning Minister de Losada made it into both *The Los Angeles Times* on July 23 and *The Washington Post* on July 25. The stories focused on the Bolivian leaders' call for more U.S. aid in that country's fight against cocaine production. *The New York Times* did not cover this story, but, instead, did two other cocaine stories on July 25. One story was out of Trinidad, Bolivia, "Bolivian Town Resents Drug Glare," and the other was a front-page metropolitan section story on "Colombian Named as Boss of 'Monster' Cocaine Ring" (in New York).

The textual analysis has indicated that weekly convergence on a story exists when a story is breaking, when coverage is at its peak, and when the story comes from a national or international source. When the newspapers all go in on a breaking story, they cover it in the same ways using the same themes and sources.

The Bolivian issue is an interesting example because it is an instance where the newspapers actually also converged on not covering a story. When *The Los Angeles Times* sat on the story one day too long, it even made efforts at appearing to be in on the breaking story, and therefore to appear as if its coverage was similar to that of the other newspapers.

Convergences on the issue can also continue after a story breaks, sometimes using the same themes and sources. For example, in the July 18 story on Bolivian vows to end cocaine trafficking, the agenda is set for all three newspapers by that country's minister of the interior. At other times, the themes and sources vary. For example, *The New York Times* continued to focus on official and authoritative sources for one of its follow-up stories on Bolivia while *The Los Angeles Times* followed its leads in the peasant communities in one of its stories. Nevertheless, it is clear that, for both the Bolivian story and the earlier use and abuse story out of the National Institute on Drug Abuse, when national leaders speak, most newspapers do listen and report.

These findings hold true even when we take a look at a week we might refer to as a "valley." For example, the lowest period of coverage during which three of the four newspapers covered the cocaine story occurred during weeks 28 (October 5–11, 1986) and 30 (October 19–25). Although during these weeks *The New York Times, The Washington Post*, and *The Los Angeles Times* each ran only one cocaine story, two of these three stories were on the same theme and used the same national sources.

INTERMEDIA AGENDA-SETTING PROCESSES

Intermedia agenda-setting relationships are complex, and they represent only one aspect of the agenda-setting process. Methodologically, we have attempted to move away from simple cross-sectional analyses of the various media to tracing the dynamic process of changing media coverage over time. In their review of the factors affecting media agendas, Rogers and Dearing (1988) left no room for influences from sources who seek to purposefully influence media agendas. Therefore we propose adding sources as a factor in media agenda setting.

In chapters 5 and 6, we have looked at how the media influence each other, that is, how the media themselves set each other's agendas. However, it is clear that, although the media do seem to affect each other's coverage decisions, they also respond to events and prominent sources in a complicated cycle of convergence on a single issue. There are a variety of processes that contribute to the news media product: structural limitations, economic imperatives, and social and ideological factors, and all of these processes operate to set the news agenda. Nevertheless, we have at least begun to demonstrate that the media did converge on the drug issue in 1986, both in amount and type of coverage, and that the media themselves are important factors in setting each others' agendas.

We found that *The New York Times* sometimes acted as a leader for the other media's cocaine coverage, but it was not the only one. Other news media also sometimes picked up the cocaine "tune" and led coverage during the last two-thirds of 1986. At other times, media coverage resembled a chorus, singing together in virtual harmony.

The media did "converge" on the drug issue, as viewed both over the entire study period and within specific weeks. When weekly convergence was noted, the reasons appeared to be some prominent news event outside the local beat, fueled by prominent sources. The more long-term convergence observed over several months, the total rise in media coverage, consisted of alternating attention by media organizations from one week to the next. This cycle of attention appeared to be due more to intermedia influence, or agenda setting than to prominent news events. By looking at the entire span of coverage given the drug issue, we found that these processes, both convergence in prominent events and intermedia influences, contributed to an overall crescendo of coverage.

For example, we can speculate that the individual events (such as occurred in Bolivia) might not have been given such heavy play had they not been bracketed by peaks in media coverage of the drug issue generally. And the angles, or themes, taken on Bolivia might have been different if the overall coverage of the "drug epidemic" had not primed subsequent stories. The agenda-setting model places mass communication in the center of political theory, and in a society based on pluralistic principles, how the media converge on vital public issues is an essential question. It is, essentially, a question of diversity. But the findings of convergence among the media on the themes and sources of the cocaine stories certainly do not support assumptions of diversity among the newspapers studied.

We have seen that another important question revolves around which sources get to set the media's agenda. For the cocaine story, it appeared to be mostly national leaders. This is potentially troublesome, for if we hear mostly the voices of national leaders on issues as they are first developed and defined, and if an issue becomes a story when national leaders speak, then they can frame the debate. For example, what happens when these leaders decide that the "cocaine epidemic" calls for military action in a foreign country? What other voices are heard?

These questions are becoming more important given the central role of the media in political life. Consequently, we need to be fully aware of all the factors that set the agenda of the media, causing them to converge on certain issues, sources, and themes.

REFERENCES

Altheide, D.L. (1982). Three-in-one news: Network coverage of Iran. *Journalism Quarterly, 59,* 482–86.

Baker, R. (1986, July 26). Same old junk. *New York Times,* p. 15.

Becker, L., McCombs, M., & McLeod, J. (1975). The development of political cognitions. In S. Chaffee (Ed.), *Political communication: Issues and strategies for research* (pp. 21–63). Beverly Hills, CA: Sage.

Bolivian reports were withheld. Several U.S. news groups say they delayed disclosure of anti-cocaine offensive. (1986, July 20). *The New York Times,* p. 8.

Gans, H. (1979). *Deciding what's news.* New York: Random House.

Kerr, P. (1986, November 17). Anatomy of an issue: Drugs, the evidence, the reaction. *The New York Times,* p.1.

Rogers, E.M., & Dearing, J. W. (1988). Agenda-setting research: Where has it been, where is it going. In J. Anderson (Ed.), *Communication Yearbook 11* (pp. 555–594). Beverly Hills, CA: Sage.

Sigal, L.V. (1973). *Reporters and officials. The organization and politics of newsmaking.* Lexington, MA: D.C. Heath.

7

Drug Coverage and Public Opinion, 1972–1986

Pamela J. Shoemaker
Wayne Wanta
Dawn Leggett
The University of Texas at Austin

In 1986 the American public got a big dose of drug coverage from the mass media. Newspapers, magazines, and television reacted en masse to the drug-related deaths of famous athletes, the pleas for reform from celebrities, and the information campaigns of public health agencies. The result was an unprecedented amount of media coverage of drug-caused tragedies, new illegal drugs, and the social ramifications of a drug-dependent population.

At the same time, opinion polls showed an increase in public concern about illegal drugs, and Congress wrote and passed a $1.7 billion antidrug legislation package within weeks.

Yet, as Peter Kerr's (1986) *New York Times* article pointed out, these changes in the amount of media coverage and the extent of public concern were not accompanied by a sudden increase in drug use. The problem had been steadily building since the 1960s, when the modern cycle of drug use began with the popularizing of marijuana and heroin. In the 1970s hallucinogens like LSD and PCP gained popularity, to be replaced by cocaine late in that decade. Cocaine-related deaths became frequent in the early 1980s, and the number of addicts accelerated when crack, a potent smokable form of cocaine, became available in late 1985.

Given a steadily growing problem, Kerr asked what made the media "discover" the problem in late 1985 and what made public concern suddenly grow. He cited the advent of crack, the deaths of famous athletes, and the approach of Congressional elections as three obvious reasons, but suggested that more complex causes may underlie these superficial ones.

The New York Times was not the only medium questioning the validity of the drug "wave" in the media: An early 1987 article in *TV Guide* by Edwin Diamond, Frank Accosta, and Leslie-Jean Thornton questioned the accuracy of media reports about drugs, particularly cocaine and crack. They monitored network television's crack coverage during the spring and summer of 1986. Although the number of drug stories rose dramatically through this period, the authors said, there was no evidence that the level of drug abuse had changed. "Rather, it was the level of *media reporting* of drug abuse – and, above all, of some dramatic cocaine cases – that soared and plummeted" (p. 6). Following the dramatic coverage of the summer, the fall brought a more "reflective phase," when "the media coverage of crack became a story itself" (Diamond et al., 1987, p. 6). People began to ask whether the story had been exaggerated. "ABC reporter John Quinones . . . defended the networks against charges of hype, saying that coverage was careful, though he acknowledged that 'sometimes we have a tendency to feed on one another, and the story feeds upon itself' " (Diamond et al., 1987, p. 10).

A potential danger of media hype is that the importance of the drug problem will be exaggerated in the mind of the public. This chapter investigates the relationship between changes in media coverage of drug-related issues and in public concern about drugs. The agenda-setting hypothesis (McCombs & Shaw, 1972) suggests that changes in media emphasis on an issue will be followed by changes in public concern about that issue – that the increase in public concern about illegal drugs during 1986 was at least partially caused by the increased amount of coverage that the mass media gave to drug topics. To test the agenda-setting hypothesis, we correlated the percentage of people in Gallup polls between 1972 and 1986 who said that drugs were "the most important problem facing the country today" with the number of drug-related stories in selected newspapers, television, and news magazines.

AGENDA SETTING AND DRUG ISSUES

The first use of the term *agenda setting* and the first formal test of such a hypothesis was by McCombs and Shaw (1972), although others had theorized about such a media effect or had tested similar hypotheses (see, e.g., Cohen, 1963; Funkhouser, 1973). The approach has its roots in the oldest concerns of scholars and politicians about the potential power of the press in controlling public opinion (e.g., Lasswell, 1927; LeBon, 1896/1968; Lippmann, 1922). Although early conceptions of agenda setting primarily dealt with how the *public* agenda is formed, scholars are also studying formation of both the *media* agenda and the *policy* agenda (Rogers & Dearing, 1988). Our study includes measures of media emphasis on drug issues before and after measures of public concern about drugs, allowing us to look at potential influences of the media and public agendas on each other.

Tests of the agenda-setting hypothesis have compared media and public agendas in a variety of ways. In their original study, McCombs and Shaw (1972) found almost a perfect rank-order correlation between the media (*The New York Times*, four local newspapers, *Time* and *Newsweek*) and public agendas on a variety of campaign issues during one 4-week period. Tipton, Haney, and Baseheart (1975) compared media (local newspapers, television, and radio) and public agendas on multiple issues at three times. Stone and McCombs (1981) looked at media content (*Time* and *Newsweek*) several months before and after three measures of public concern about a variety of topics. Behr and Iyengar (1985) compared concern for and media attention to inflation, unemployment, and energy between 1974 and 1980 in network television news. Winter and Eyal (1981) compared public concern with civil rights between 1954 and 1976 with civil rights coverage in *The New York Times*.

A review of the scholarly literature on media coverage of drugs reveals very little published since the mid- to late-1970s. In 1976 Schmeling and Wotring published results of an agenda-setting study of the effects of public-service ads. A 1976 book edited by Ostman offered several studies on the effects of mass communicated drug information, primarily educational in purpose, on the audience.

Cohen and Young's (1981) edited volume includes several studies from the 1970s that investigate media coverage of drugs. Braden (in Cohen & Young, 1981) said that reporters were "befuddled" by LSD and were unable to write good stories due to their lack of scientific training. Braden also pointed out that an emphasis on bad experiences with LSD was a reflection of news values: A bad trip was more newsworthy than a good trip. In the same volume, Young (1981) said that media condemnation of drug taking is a function of the deviance of illegal drugs rather than a concern with health risks. The media, Young said, interpret events within a consensual framework that leads them to frame drug taking as a moral rather than as a health issue. "By fanning up moral panics over drug use, [the media portrayal of the drug user] contributes enormously to public hostility to the drug taker and precludes any rational approach to the problem" (Young, 1981, p. 334).

But Kerr's (1986) description of the media discovery of the drug story has more in common with the "crime wave" studies described in Cohen and Young (1981), than with the LSD/media studies. Fishman (1981) described how the mass media "created" a 1976 New York City crime wave by the way in which they organized and selected news to be presented to the public. Fishman defined *crime wave* as a "social awareness of crime, crime brought to the public consciousness" (p. 98). Although a crime wave cannot mug anyone, it can scare people and encourage the enactment of new laws. Ten years later, Kerr (1986) seemed to suggest, we saw the occurrence of a "drug wave"—an increase in the social awareness of drugs at least partially caused by the mass media.

Our study tests the extent to which shifts in the media emphasis on drugs over 15 years correlates with shifts in public concern about drugs during the same time frame. Our first hypothesis is, simply, that the more the media emphasize drugs, the more people will list drugs as the most important problem facing the country. This is the basic agenda-setting hypothesis, which assumes that causality runs from the media agenda to the public agenda; however, we also test reverse causality.

Our second hypothesis deals with differences among the mass media. Although the absolute amount of coverage is expected to differ among newspapers, television, and news magazines, we hypothesize that changes in coverage of drugs over time will occur similarly among the three types of media. We assume that newspaper, network television, and news magazine content is influenced by similar basic conceptions of newsworthiness, thereby resulting in similar decisions about how newsworthy drug stories are at different points in time.

Our third hypothesis deals with the time lag between changes in the media agenda and the public agenda. Winter and Eyal (1981) suggest that the "optimal effect span" is between 4 and 6 weeks, whereas Stone and McCombs (1981) suggest that it takes 2 to 6 months for changes in the media agenda to be fully "translated" to the public agenda. Our hypothesis is a compromise between the two predictions—that the largest observed relationship between media and public agendas will be when the media agenda is measured 2 months prior to the measurement of the public agenda.

METHOD

Our study method is based on that used by Winter and Eyal (1981). We determined public concern with drugs from 46 Gallup polls conducted between 1972 and 1986 that asked the question "What is the most important problem facing this country today?"

We measured changes in media emphasis on drugs by counting the number of stories dealing with illegal drugs in indexes for *The New York Times, The Chicago Tribune, The Los Angeles Times, Time, Newsweek, U.S. News and World Report,* ABC evening news, NBC evening news, and CBS evening news. The *Vanderbilt Archives News Abstracts* was used to measure network television emphasis of drug issues. *Reader's Guide to the Periodical Literature* was used to measure the news magazines' emphasis of drug issues. Each newspaper's own index was used for its measurement. Every story dealing with illegal drugs was counted by first turning to all "drug" headings in each index, then by following references to additional drug-related headings. Duplicate references to the same story were eliminated.

Measurements of each medium's agenda were made by counting the number of stories in each of the 6 months immediately prior to each Gallup poll and 1 month immediately following each poll. Thus the "poll" is our unit of analysis, with a sample size of 46. Because each Gallup poll was conducted over 3 days, we arbitrarily used the middle day of data collection as the basis for determining when "1 month" began and ended (e.g., if the poll was conducted between April 10–12, then 1 month prior to the poll was defined as March 11–April 10 for the purpose of measuring media content). Intercoder reliability of story counts assessed on a sample of stories from all of the media was .93.

We used the "number of stories about illegal drugs" as our measure of the media agenda instead of the length of the stories for practical reasons: Given a finite amount of time for data collection, measuring column inches of print stories would have required that we reduce the number of media under study from nine to only one or two. In addition, Stone and McCombs (1981) found a Pearson correlation coefficient of $+.90$ between the number of stories and the number of column inches devoted to a variety of topics, indicating that the easier measurement may be as good a predictor.

Our study goes beyond Winter and Eyal (1981) by adding two newspapers, three television networks, and three news magazines to the analysis, as well as measurement of the media agenda 1 month following each poll. Therefore we are able to generalize our results beyond one elite newspaper, and we are able to test reverse causality running from the public agenda to the media agenda.

Some of the analyses we performed used aggregated television, newspaper, and news magazine indexes created by summing the three scores within each type of medium. Cronbach's alpha for the newspaper indexes were: 6 months prior to poll, .52; 5 months prior, .49; 4 months prior, .50; 3 months prior, .48; 2 months prior, .45; 1 month prior, .51. Cronbach's alpha for the television indexes were: 6 months prior, .88; 5 months prior, .85; 4 months prior, .86; 3 months prior, .91; 2 months prior, .88; 1 month prior, .91. Cronbach's alpha for the news magazine indexes were: 6 months prior, .59; 5 months prior, .40; 4 months prior, .59; 3 months prior, .70; 2 months prior, .66; 1 month prior, .44. The higher reliability figures for the television indexes indicate more similarity in drug coverage among the television networks than among the other media.

RESULTS

Gallup polls provide estimates of the percentage of Americans rating drugs as the most important problem facing the country. Of the years under study (1972 through 1986), public concern with drugs was highest in the early 1970s, became very low during the late 1970s and early 1980s, and climbed again in 1985 and 1986 (Table 7.1).

Media coverage also varied over those 15 years and in much the same pattern. We looked at *The New York Times, The Chicago Tribune, The Los Angeles Times, Time, Newsweek, U.S. News & World Report,* ABC evening news, NBC evening news, and CBS evening news. Table 7.1 shows that the mean number of drug stories in the 6 months preceding each poll was highest in the early 1970s and the mid 1980s.

Hypothesis 1 stated that the more the media emphasize drugs, the more people will list drugs as the most important problem facing the country. Table 7.2 shows Pearson correlation coefficients for each media measure with the percentage of respondents listing drugs as the most important problem facing America. The media variables measure the monthly number of stories from each medium from 1 to 6 months preceding each Gallup poll and for 1 month following each poll. The correlation coefficients are nearly all positive, with the exception of those for *Time* magazine, confirming the similarities observed in Table 7.1 between changes in poll and media data and providing some support for hypothesis one.

Additional tests of hypothesis one are presented in Table 7.3. Because of the small number of cases (46 polls), the data for a given time period were aggregated within each medium, and we used the media indexes described at the end of the method section. The dependent variable was the percentage of people who listed "drugs" as the most important problem facing the country. The media variables entered the regression equation hierarchically, with media coverage 1 month prior to the poll entering first and coverage 6 months prior to the poll entering last. Table 7.3 supports hypothesis 1, showing that half of the variance (adjusted R^2) in the poll data can be accounted for by the cumulative coverage in these nine media during the 6 months prior to the polls.

Hypothesis 2 predicted that changes in coverage of drugs over time would occur similarly among the three types of media. Of the three newspapers, *The New York Times'* and *The Los Angeles Times'* coverage showed the strongest relationship to the poll data, and *The New York Times'* coverage was more strongly related to the poll data than was that of any other medium in the study. Although we had expected the three newspapers to cover drugs similarly, *The Chicago Tribune's* coverage of drugs was unrelated to the public opinion poll data.

TABLE 7.1
Changes in Media and Public Agendas, 1972–1986

Year	Number of Gallup Polls in That Year	Mean % Respondents Citing Drugs as "Most Important Problem"	Mean # Television Stories in 6 Months Prior to Polls	Mean # Newspaper Stories in 6 Months Prior to Polls	Mean # News Magazine Stories in 6 Months Prior to Polls
1972	2	9.0	57	918	17
1973	3	15.3	74	933	13
1974	4	1.0	35	622	6
1975	3	.7	40	467	6
1976	3	1.0	41	384	4
1977	3	1.3	31	366	5
1978	3	1.0	41	356	4
1979	3	0	38	304	5
1980	4	0	52	275	12
1981	2	0	42	287	13
1982	4	0	45	377	16
1983	3	0	106	551	22
1984	4	.3	107	670	25
1985	3	3.7	128	545	22
1986	2	5.0	113	609	29

TABLE 7.2
Pearson Correlation Coefficients for Percentage of Public Citing "Drugs" as the
"Most Important Problem Facing America Today" with Media Coverage of
Drugs Before Each Poll, ($N = 46$)

Period Before Gallup Polls	Media		
	The New York Times	The Chicago Tribune	The Los Angeles Times
6 months before	.46***	.22	.50***
5 months before	.57***	.07	.61***
4 months before	.67***	.09	.52***
3 months before	.49***	.12	.49***
2 months before	.56***	.12	.57***
1 month before	.73***	.11	.30*
	Time	Newsweek	US News & World Report
6 months before	−.07	.38**	.08
5 months before	−.18	.20	.11
4 months before	−.06	.29*	.22
3 months before	−.03	.02	−.08
2 months before	.12	.21	.11
1 month before	−.03	.29*	.04
	ABC	CBS	NBC
6 months before	.09	.21	.10
5 months before	.17	.26*	.08
4 months before	.35**	.24*	.09
3 months before	.17	.08	−.01
2 months before	.12	.19	−.01
1 month before	.36**	.19	.23*

*$p < .05$
**$p < .01$
***$p < .001$

Of the three news magazines, the drug coverage of *Time* and *U.S. News & World Report* was unrelated to public opinion on drugs. Drug coverage in *Newsweek* was related to public opinion in months 1, 4, and 6 preceding the Gallup polls, although the correlation coefficients are small.

Of the three television networks, NBC's coverage was unrelated to the public opinion measures, except in the month immediately preceding the polls. ABC and CBS fared better, with two instances each where coverage (for CBS, months 4 and 5; for ABC, months 1 and 4) was correlated with public opinion.

Therefore, we conclude that hypothesis 2 is not supported. The newspapers were most strongly related to the poll data, with the televi-

TABLE 7.3
Hierarchical Regression Analysis of Media Agenda Variables on Public Concern
With Drugs ($N = 46$)

Independent Variable Blocks[a]	Std. Beta[b]	R^2 Change	Total R^2	Adjusted R^2
1. Newspaper – 1 month before poll	.65*			
Television	.16			
News magazine	.03	.44***	.44***	.40
2. Newspaper – 2 months before poll	−.49			
Television	.19			
News magazine	.23	.01	.45***	.36
3. Newspaper – 3 months before poll	−.45			
Television	.38			
News magazine	−.40*	.07	.52***	.40
4. Newspaper – 4 months before poll	.87*			
Television	.10			
News magazine	−.35	.12*	.64***	.51
5. Newspaper – 5 months before poll	.61			
Television	−.35			
News magazine	−.09	.04	.68***	.52
6. Newspaper – 6 months before poll	−.26			
Television	−.19			
News magazine	−.08	.02	.70***	.50

[a]The independent variables are the indexes created by summing scores within each time frame for the three newspapers, for the three television networks, and for the three news magazines.

[b]Standardized betas are taken from the final step in the regression analysis, when all variables are in the equation.

*$p < .05$
**$p < .01$
***$p < .001$

sion networks being second and the news magazines third. However, within each type of medium, there was considerable variance among how strongly the specific media were related to the poll data. The strongest relationships were observed with *The New York Times, The Los Angeles Times,* CBS evening news, ABC evening news, and *Newsweek.*

Table 7.4 shows additional analyses we performed to determine the relative contributions of the nine media to explaining variance in public concern with drugs. Table 7.4 describes the results of a stepwise regression analysis, in which an index was constructed for each medium by adding the number of stories each medium transmitted about drugs during months 1 through 6 preceding each poll. Cronbach's alpha for *The New York Times* was, .96; for *The Los Angeles Times,* .92; for *The Chicago Tribune,* .91; for *Time,* .54; for *Newsweek,* .65; for *U.S. News & World Report,* .20; for ABC evening news, .68; for NBC evening news, .69; for CBS evening news, .72.

As Table 7.4 shows, nearly half of the variance in public concern with

TABLE 7.4
Stepwise Regression Analysis of Drug Coverage by Nine Media on Public
Concern With Drugs ($N = 46$)

Medium[a]	Std. Beta[b]	R^2 Change	Total R^2	Adjusted R^2
The New York Times	.45**	.38***	.40***	.38
The Los Angeles Times	.35**	.09**	.48***	.46

Note: The other media did not enter the regression equation due to low tolerance. They are:
The Chicago Tribune
Time
Newsweek
U.S. News & World Report
ABC evening news
NBC evening news
CBS evening news
[a]An index was created for each medium by summing the amount of drug coverage in each of the 6 months immediately preceding each poll.
[b]Standardized betas were taken from the final step in the regression equation.
*$p < .05$
**$p < .01$
***$p < .001$

drugs (adjusted R^2) can be explained by only two of the nine media we studied—*The New York Times* and *The Los Angeles Times*. In the stepwise regression analysis, none of the other seven media entered the regression equation, due to those variables' low tolerance.

Hypothesis 3 deals with the time lag between changes in the media agenda and the public agenda. We hypothesized a compromise (of 2 months) between Winter and Eyal's (1981) suggestion that 4 to 6 weeks is optimal and Stone and McCombs' (1981) suggestion that 2 to 6 months is optimal. Table 7.3 shows that the media coverage in the 4 weeks immediately preceding the poll accounts for 40% (adjusted R^2) of the variance in poll data, and that only month 4 media coverage adds a statistically significant amount to R^2.

A look at the Pearson correlation coefficients in Table 7.2 confirms the existence of these two important time periods. For four of the nine media studied, the largest correlation coefficients are seen in months 1 and 4 preceding the polls. For two media, the largest coefficients are in months 2 and 5. In Table 7.3, we see that months 1 and 4 together account for 80% of the (unadjusted R^2) variance explained by all 6 months' media coverage.

So, for coverage of illegal drugs, there are apparently two important time periods during which media coverage affects public opinion data—1 or 2 months prior to the measurement of public opinion and 4 or 5 months prior to the poll. It may be the recurring nature of the topic that has the most effect on public opinion. Therefore, our hypothesis about a compromise between the two previously published estimates of the optimum relationship between public opinion and media coverage was not supported. Instead, we find evidence in favor of both of the previous predictions: There are two time periods in which media coverage correlates highly with public opinion.

We are also able to look at the relationship between the poll data and media coverage after the polls. Table 7.5 shows the Pearson correlation coefficients between public opinion and media coverage within 1 month following the polls, as well as first- and second-order partial coefficients controlling for media coverage in the first and fourth months prior to the poll. We see statistically significant zero-order correlation coefficients for four of the nine media studied. In the cases of *The New York Times, The Los Angeles Times,* and ABC evening news, the relationships probably represent continuing interest on the part of these media; their coverage of drugs was also related to the poll data in the month immediately preceding the poll. In the case of CBS evening news, there was no relationship between coverage and the poll data immediately before the poll, so the relationship between coverage and poll data after the poll may be evidence of the CBS agenda being set by the poll and by coverage by other media. The same process may be occurring with *The Chicago Tribune* and with *U.S. News & World Report*; although the coefficients are not statistically significant, they are much larger in the month following the poll than in the month immediately preceding it.

Controlling for media coverage in the first and fourth months prior to the poll (Table 7.5) yields nonsignificant second-order partial correlation coefficients for all nine media, supporting our sense that media coverage after a poll is best explained by media coverage before the poll.

In summary, hypothesis 1 was supported by the data, showing clear evidence for an agenda-setting effect of the nine media studied on public concern with drugs. Hypotheses 2 and 3 were not supported: There was no evidence of similarity in coverage among the media; in fact, two of the newspapers accounted for almost all of the total effect of these nine media on public concern with drugs. In addition, there was evidence for media agenda-setting effects in two time periods—during the weeks immediately preceding the poll and during a second period about 3 months earlier.

DISCUSSION

Our study was designed to test the relationship between changes in media coverage of drugs over 15 years and changes in public concern with drugs. We correlated the number of drug stories in three newspapers, three television networks' evening news shows, and three news magazines

TABLE 7.5

Zero-Order Pearson Correlation Coefficients (and Partial Coefficients Controlling for Coverage 1 Month and 4 Months Prior to the Poll) for Percentage of Public Citing "Drugs" as the "Most Important Problem Facing America Today" With Media Coverage of Drugs in the 1 Month Immediately Following Each Poll ($N = 46$)

Medium	Zero-Order Pearson r	First-Order Partial r, Controlling for Coverage in First Month Prior to Poll	First-Order Partial r, Controlling for Coverage in Fourth Month Prior to Poll	Second-Order Partial r, Controlling for Coverage in First & Fourth Months Prior to Poll
The New York Times	.72***	.26*	.42**	.23
The Chicago Tribune	.22	−.11	.03	−.11
The Los Angeles Times	.35**	.19	.13	.14
Time	.00	.00	−.01	−.01
Newsweek	.15	.02	−.03	−.07
US News & World Report	.22	.23	.14	.14
ABC	.30*	.09	.21	.10
CBS	.27*	.22	.22	.19
NBC	.18	.07	.17	.07

*$p < .05$
**$p < .01$
***$p < .001$

with Gallup poll data on the percentage of respondents who list drugs as the most important problem facing America today. The results show evidence in favor of the agenda-setting hypothesis: The more the mass media emphasize drugs, the more the public is concerned with drugs as a problem.

Despite self-criticism of the mass media about exaggerating the drug problem, our data show that newspaper drug coverage in the 6 months immediately preceding each Gallup poll was higher in the early 1970s than in 1986, the year that precipitated so much concern about media exaggeration of drugs. Drug coverage in the three television networks and in the three news magazines, however, was about twice as high in 1986 as it had been in the early 1970s.

Although drug coverage in the nine media accounted for half of the variance in public concern with drugs over the 15 years, the media did not contribute equally to the relationship. Newspapers were the most important in explaining variance in the Gallup poll data, but they were not equally important. Of the three major, big-city newspapers we studied, *The Chicago Tribune*'s drug coverage was unrelated to public concern with drugs, whereas *The New York Times* and *The Los Angeles Times* were responsible for almost all of the variance in public opinion accounted for by all nine media. These two major newspapers may have had more influence on public concern with drugs than do all three major television networks and all three major news magazines combined.

Agenda-setting studies nearly always seem concerned with the time frame over which media coverage has the most impact on public opinion, and ours is no exception. We are able to test the relationship between media coverage and public opinion in each of the 6 months immediately preceding each poll. The largest bivariate relationships were observed in the first month or two immediately before the poll and again in the fourth or fifth months before the poll. Hierarchical regression analysis, putting the months into the equation in chronological order beginning with the first month before the poll, showed that months 1 and 4 were the keys, accounting for more than three-fourths of all of the variance explained. This suggests that coverage which recurs in emphasis on a 3- or 4-month schedule may have the most influence on public opinion.

REFERENCES

Behr, R.L., & Iyengar, S. (1985). Television news, real-world cues, and changes in the public agenda. *Public Opinion Quarterly, 49,* 38–57.

Braden, W. (1981). LSD and the press. In S. Cohen & J. Young (Eds.), *The manufacture of news* (pp. 248–262). Beverly Hills, CA: Sage.

Cohen, B.C. (1963). *The press and foreign policy.* Princeton, NJ: Princeton University Press.

Cohen, S., & Young, J. (1981). *The manufacture of news.* Beverly Hills, CA: Sage.

Diamond, E., Accosta, F., & Thornton, L. (1987, February 7). Is TV news hyping America's cocaine problem? *TV Guide,* pp. 4–10.

Fishman, M. (1981). Crime waves as ideology. In S. Cohen & J. Young (Eds.), *The manufacture of news* (pp. 98–117). Beverly Hills, CA: Sage.

Funkhouser, G.R. (1973). The issues of the sixties: An exploratory study in the dynamics of public opinion. *Public Opinion Quarterly, 37,* 62–75.

Kerr, P. (1986, November 17). Anatomy of an issue: Drugs, the evidence, the reaction, *New York Times,* pp. 1, 12.

Lasswell, H. D. (1927). *Propaganda technique in the world war.* New York: Knopf.

LeBon, G. (1968). *The crowd.* Dunwoody, GA: Norman S. Berg. (Originally published 1896).

Lippmann, W. (1922). *Public Opinion.* New York: Harcourt Brace.

McCombs, M.E. & Shaw, D. L. (1972). The agenda-setting function of mass media. *Public Opinion Quarterly, 36,* 176–184.

Ostman, R.,E. (Ed.). (1976). *Communication research and drug education.* Beverly Hills, CA: Sage.

Rogers, E.M., & Dearing, J.W. (1988). Agenda-setting research: Where has it been, where is it going? In J. Anderson (Ed.), *Communication Yearbook 11* (pp. 555–594). Beverly Hills, CA: Sage.

Schmeling, D.G., & Wotring, C.E. (1976). Agenda-setting effects of drug-abuse public-service ads. *Journalism Quarterly, 53,* 743–746.

Stone, G.C., & McCombs, M.E. (1981). Tracing the time lag in agenda-setting. *Journalism Quarterly, 58,* 51–55.

Tipton, L., Haney, R.D., & Baseheart, J.R. (1975). Media agenda-setting in city and state election campaigns. *Journalism Quarterly, 52,* 15–22.

Winter, J.P., & Eyal, C.H. (1981). Agenda setting for the civil rights issue. *Public Opinion Quarterly, 45,* 376–383.

Young, J. (1981). The myth of drug takers in the mass media. In S. Cohen & J. Young (Eds.), *The manufacture of news* (pp. 326–334). Beverly Hills, CA: Sage.

8

Citizen Attitudes Toward Drug Testing: Value Conflict or Consensus?

Dorothy Davidson Nesbit
DDB Needham Worldwide Inc., Chicago

This chapter examines public attitudes in Illinois on drug testing during a period of intense media coverage. It is limited in that media content is not measured as systematically as are public attitudes and media exposure is not directly linked to individual attitudes. However, it can indirectly provide insights into the role of the media in shaping public attitudes and perceptions, increase our understanding of the behavior of policymakers on highly exposed issues, and contribute to the discussion of how to define or prescribe the limits of public opinion on policy.

Public debate on drug testing has focused on four central issues—public health and safety, accuracy, privacy, and cost. Perhaps the most persuasive argument for testing is that it is essential for the protection of public health and safety. One argument in favor of drug testing cites the potential for substance abuse among physicians, transportation workers, and others who have major responsibility for the public safety. For example, a Pulitzer Prize-winning series of articles published by *The Pittsburgh Press* documented a frightening abuse of alcohol and drug abuse among airline pilots (Brelis & Schneider, 1986a, 1986b; Schneider, 1986a, 1986b, 1986c, 1986d, 1986e, 1986f; Schneider & Bowman, 1986; Schneider & Brelis, 1986a, 1986b). Other advocates of testing note that the potential for blackmail and the compromise of the national defense exists if government workers who have access to national security information are also substance abusers.

For a number of reasons, some people remain unconvinced by these arguments. In particular, opponents of drug testing have expressed concern about the accuracy of test results. A study of 13 laboratories by the federal Centers for Disease Control in Atlanta showed an error rate of up to 66% (Gest, 1985). A false positive urinalysis could ruin careers, disrupt personal lives, and destroy reputations. A false negative could defeat the whole purpose of testing by allowing substance abusers to go undetected. According to a study released by the United States House of Representatives civil service subcommittee and Representative Patricia Schroeder, random testing of the federal work force could jeopardize the careers of 140,000 to 500,000 employees with false positive results. The results would be on their records, and the employees would be forced to deal with them for the rest of their lives (Thornton, 1986).

James Woodford, an Atlanta forensic chemist, noted that minorities may be more at risk from inaccurate tests than the white population. His research indicates that dark skin pigmentations are more likely to yield "false positive" results—and thus the tests may be discriminatory (Lindsey, 1986). The falsification of urine samples is also a possibility unless collection of urine is unannounced in advance of the test and urine samples are delivered under observation.

Observed collection of urine raises issues of modesty and good taste, as well as of privacy. The privacy issue is a complex legal and constitutional question. Individuals are protected under the fourth amendment to the U.S. Constitution against search and seizure without probable cause, although this prohibition applies only to the government and not to private employers. Testing circumstances may violate an individual's protection against self-incrimination, as well as other civil rights. The administration of drug tests, and an employer's actions based on the results of drug tests, have already provided the impetus for legal action. In 13 of 17 testing-related law suits filed against the government between January 1985 and December 1986, state and federal judges ruled that random drug testing is unconstitutional unless the authorities have "reasonable suspicion" or "probable cause" to believe that people have used drugs. In only four cases were random drug tests found constitutionally permissible (Kerr, 1986).

The social costs of a drug-testing policy are but one dimension of the total policy costs; the financial costs are not insignificant. In order to provide protection against inaccurate results, some mechanism for retesting employees who initially test positive may be required. The more sophisticated tests may cost as much as $100 per analysis. In addition, because testing implies some action will be based on the results, employers may also provide referrals or treatment programs for those who test (and retest) as positive. The cost of testing and retesting and of providing treatment referrals and employee assistance programs will increase the financial burden on companies that undertake drug testing. Additional indirect costs of drug testing include productivity lost while tests are being conducted and problems due to the potentially negative impact of testing on employee morale.

Among the reasons that legislators are now addressing the drug-testing issue is their assumption that drug testing has broad public support. Indeed, some legislators might interpret the available evidence to suggest that the public demands drug testing. How can policymakers evaluate public attitudes toward drug testing in the workplace and arrive at a politically feasible response? Should political feasibility be a key consideration in a policy domain characterized by important constitutional issues? Is public support for drug testing widespread and strong, or is it thin and unstable and therefore fraught with risk for political actors?

The analyses in this chapter use data from a statewide survey conducted in Illinois. Illinois is considered a microcosm of the United States by many journalists and pollsters (Braden, 1986; CBS/*New York Times* Poll, 1986). As such, it is often used as a test market for new products or marketing ideas. Illinois is also a popular spot for testing the political waters by those running for national office. Four questions are examined with respect to public opinion on drug testing. What is the extent of public concern about drug abuse? What is the level of public approval for administering drug tests to different kinds of workers? What are the impacts of accuracy and privacy issues on support for testing? How willing is the public to pay the social costs of a drug-testing policy?

METHOD

Since the Spring of 1984, the Center for Governmental Studies at Northern Illinois University has been conducting statewide studies of public attitudes toward political issues. The results reported here are based on 700 interviews conducted October 16–27, 1986. The Public Opinion Laboratory at NIU performed the interviewing and sampling for the study.

Sampling procedures used in this study allowed each telephone exchange in Illinois a proportionate probability of selection. The number of households within a prefix is directly proportionate to the number of residential mainstations in that prefix. Strict guidelines were set for the selection and replacement of numbers.

At each residence that contained an eligible respondent, the person to be interviewed was selected randomly. Eligible respondents were 18 years of age or older and residents of Illinois. Selection was accomplished by a computer routine that randomly chooses from among adults enumerated by age. If the selected respondent was not at home, a callback appointment was arranged. Substitution of respondents was not allowed.

Up to three callbacks were made in an attempt to reach the selected respondent. The combined result of these procedures is a representative statewide sample of the Illinois adult population accessible by telephone.

The data were weighted to restore equal probability of selection. The weighting formula included an adjustment for the number of adults in the household and the number of different phone numbers in the household.

The completion rate for the survey was 75%. The CASRO response rate was 34%. Study documentation can be obtained from the Center for Governmental Studies at Northern Illinois University or by writing to the author.

RESULTS

The question of drug testing by employers affects the public and private sectors very differently. The private sector is not bound by the fourth amendment to the Constitution. However, neither sector is exempt from the high price of legal fees and employee good will if the tests are not conducted accurately, fairly, and with proper respect for the individual.

The Need for Drug Testing in the Workplace

According to Leonard Glantz (1986), professor at health law of Boston University, the issues of protecting public health and random drug testing are quite separate. He noted that the proposed drug tests are for illegal drugs, but that legal drugs (including alcohol, prescription drugs, and over-the-counter medications) can impair mental acuity. Furthermore, the fact that one has metabolites of drugs present in urine does not establish impairment. The metabolites traces remain for days and even weeks after the intoxicating effects have worn off.

In attempting to garner support for mandatory drug testing of federal employees, President Ronald Reagan proudly handed over a urine specimen for analysis in August 1986. Vice President George Bush's appointment to deliver his sample followed closely behind—prompting Washington columnist William Safire to comment that the vice president's test indicated that he had "neither a drug addiction nor a mind of his own" (Safire, 1986, p. 8).

Most people would probably agree that it is desirable for workers, especially the chief executive and his staff, to be unimpaired by any substance that might affect their judgment. Few, if any, seriously expected the White House samples to yield anything other than drug-free results. (Just as no one seriously expected Nancy Reagan to join in the "jar wars," despite the fact that she has been a leader in the White House antidrug campaign.) The need for drug testing in the workplace centers on the argument that such testing will protect public health and safety. No systematic studies have yet demonstrated that drug-impaired judgment in the workplace is a pervasive threat to the public safety. Indeed, the current campaign for a drug-testing policy appears to be predicated on the sensational instances of drug-related accidents reported by the news media.[1] Is illegal drug use pervasive in the workplace? If so, we might conclude that incidences of drug-impaired work performance are a preeminent threat to public health and safety and that such a policy is warranted.

Direct questioning of Illinois residents reveals that there is a great deal of concern about drugs. However, this concern varies substantially depending on whether the referent is the country as a whole or the more immediate environment of the respondent—such as local schools, neighborhoods, or the workplace. Respondents were told that the survey would cover a range of subjects. Early in the interview, before any other drug questions were asked, respondents were asked: "Generally speaking, would you say that drugs are the most important problem, a serious problem but other things are worse, or not much of a problem in (a) the country as a whole, (b) the state of Illinois, (c) your community, (d) your neighborhood, (e) your local schools, (f) your workplace?

Figure 8.1 shows citizen's ratings of the seriousness of the drug problem in each of these six different realms. The results suggest that citizen concerns about drug abuse are greatest with respect to the realms most removed from their daily experience. For example, 27% of those questioned believed that drugs are the most important problem in the country as a whole, whereas only 10% felt that drugs are the most important problem in their neighborhoods. Only 3% indicated that drugs are the most important problem in their workplaces.

Even if we combine the respondents who stated that drugs are a "serious problem, but other things are worse," with those who felt that drugs are the "most important problem," the decline in concern across the six realms is still striking.[2] A full 96% of the respondents said that drugs are a serious or the most important problem in the country as a whole. Only 15% said that drugs are a serious or most important problem in their

---

[1]See, for example, the Pulitzer Prize-winning series of articles published by *The Pittsburgh Press,* (Schneider, 1986a, 1986b, 1986c, 1986d, 1986e, 1986f). These articles revealed that, in a survey of 17 clinics across the country, 69 pilots had been treated for addiction without the knowledge of the Federal Aeronautics Administration (FAA). The reporters also found that the requirements for the FAA medical exam for pilots are so limited that physicians complain that they cannot detect drug or alcohol impairments.

[2]A study conducted by Johnston, Bachman, and O'Malley (1986) indicates that drug use is declining among students.

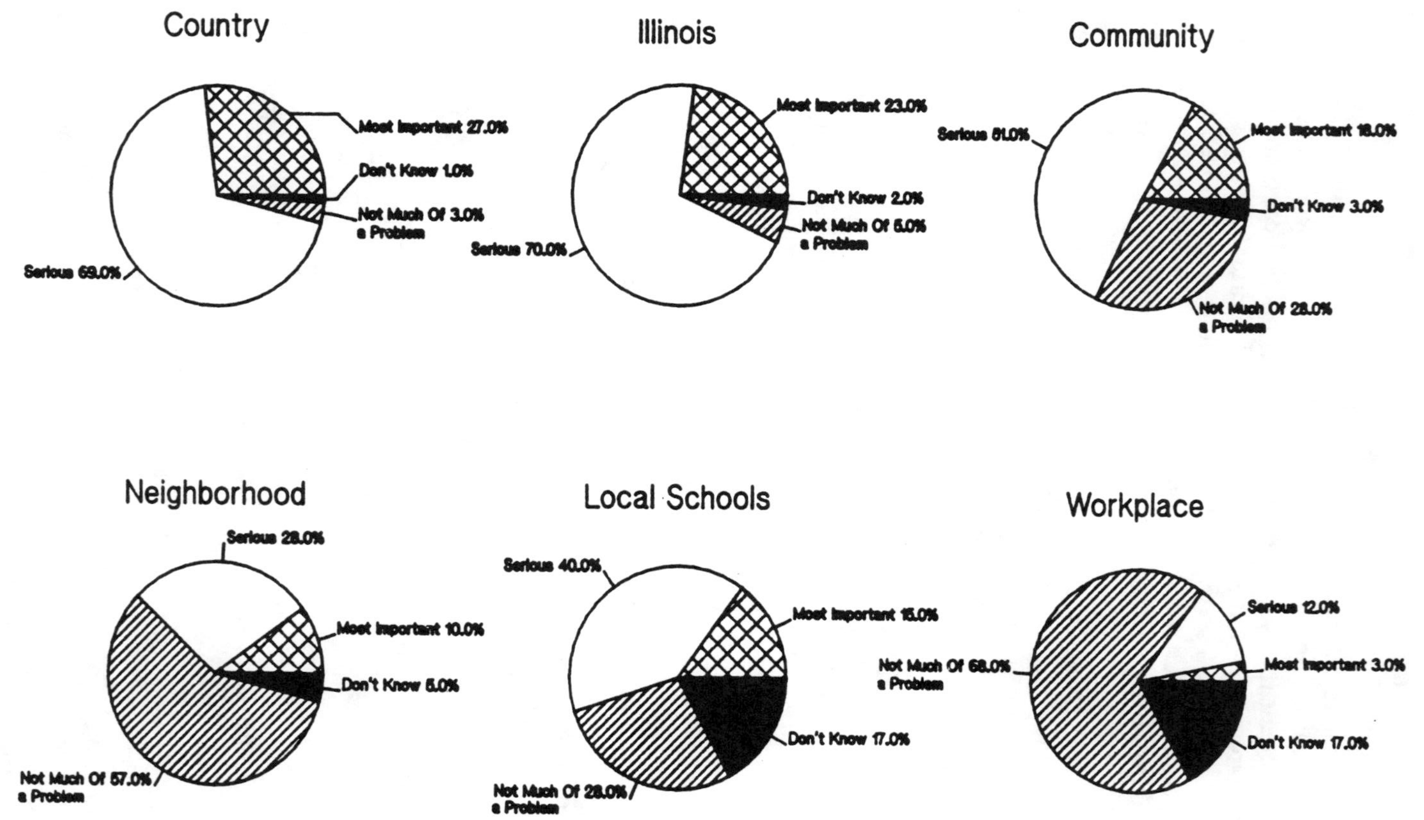

FIG. 8.1. Citizen perceptions of the drug problem in six domains ($n=700$).

workplace. Concern about drugs is greatest for the country as a whole, the state of Illinois, the community as a whole, and the local schools. There is substantially less concern about drugs in the neighborhood or workplace, and these are precisely the realms about which the respondents should have the most first-hand knowledge.[3]

Of particular interest are the 15% who indicated that drugs are either the most important or a serious problem in their workplaces. What type of work are these individuals engaged in? Simple contingency table analysis reveals that there is no relationship between income and degree of concern about drugs in the workplace. There is only a modest relationship between education and concern, with citizens having a high school education or some college exhibiting greater concern. There is no statistically significant relationship between race and concern about drugs in the workplace.

Only 75 of the 445 employed respondents indicated that drugs were the most important or a serious problem in their workplaces, making analysis by occupation inconclusive. Of those 75 respondents, 23 were professional, technical, managerial, or administrative workers; 22 were sales or clerical workers; 23 were craftsmen or operatives; 4 were service workers; and 1 was a nonfarm laborer. The number of cases in each of these groups is too small for reliable comparison.

Our conclusion from these results is that citizens are concerned about illegal drug use, but few consider it to be a problem in their immediate work environments. Existing public concern is a more globalized phenomenon that clearly does not stem from on-the-job experience. Is drug-impaired job performance a preeminent threat to the public health? Our data suggest that it is not, but that extensive coverage of drug abuse in the mass media has apparently convinced large numbers of people that the drug problem is far more serious and pervasive than their personal experiences suggest.

Public Approval of Testing and Test Accuracy

One way of assessing the stability of public support for drug testing is to introduce conditions under which testing may occur, measuring support for testing under each condition. Because one of the major arguments against a testing policy is that the tests are inaccurate, it is important to know how accurate citizens believe the tests are, and how their support for testing changes when they are given specific information about the accuracy of tests.

Prior to measuring support for drug testing, citizens were asked

---

[3]These results mirror the findings of the quality of life studies that have been conducted by others (see, e.g., Campbell, 1978).

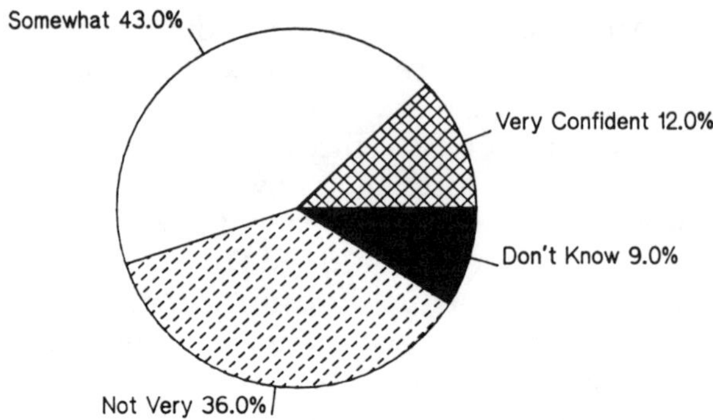

FIG. 8.2. Citizen confidence in accuracy of drug tests ($n=700$).

whether they are very confident, somewhat confident, or not very confident about the accuracy of drug tests. Figure 8.2 shows that only 12% indicated that they are very confident. More than one third are not very confident; 43% are only somewhat confident and 9% said that they "didn't know."

Although 68% of the respondents reported that drug abuse is not much of a problem in their workplace and more than one third do not have much faith in the accuracy of drug tests, overall public support for drug testing is high. Nearly 90% favored drug testing in some form.

Figure 8.3 shows that:

- 85% favor drug testing for people who are responsible for the safety of others, such as surgeons, airline pilots, and police officers

- 76% favor drug testing when there is a reasonable suspicion of abuse on the job

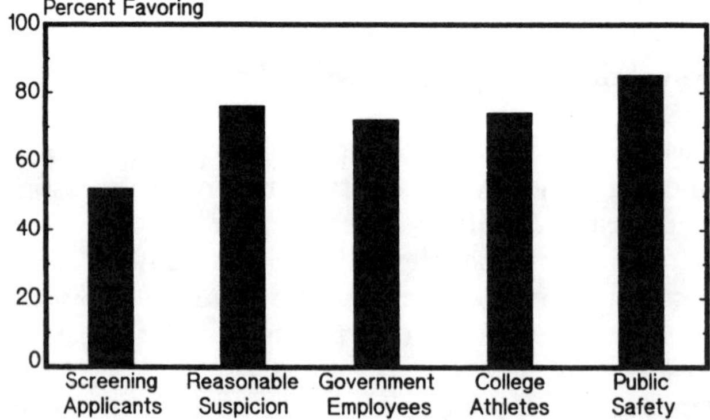

FIG. 8.3. Citizen support for drug testing in the workplace ($n=700$).

- 74% favor testing for athletes

- 72% favor testing for government employees

- 52% support allowing employers to screen job applicants for drug and alcohol use.

The largest margin of support for drug testing occurs when public safety is most explicitly jeopardized (i.e., for airline pilots, surgeons, and police officers) and when there is a reasonable suspicion of drug usage on the job. The relatively high incidence of support for testing athletes may stem from public concern about the impact on youths for whom athletes may be role models; our survey closely followed the cocaine-related death of basketball star Len Bias. The least support for drug testing, but still supported by a majority of respondents, was for using drug tests to screen job applicants. In this instance, the connection between testing and ensuring the public health is weak, and the potential harm from test inaccuracy is great.

These high levels of support for drug testing turn out to be extremely unstable. That is, respondents who initially support testing withdraw support in the face of information regarding test inaccuracy or when told that urine specimens may be delivered under observation. The 87% of citizens who favored testing in some form were subsequently asked if they would still support drug testing if they knew that as many as 6 of 10 tests are inaccurate.[4] Respondents were not told the source for this estimate, which came from the Centers for Disease Control (Gest, 1985). When confronted with this estimate about the inaccuracy of drug testing 76% of those who initially favored drug testing withdrew their support. Only 24% of respondents continued to favor drug testing, regardless of the tests' accuracy (Fig. 8.4).

We speculated that political conservatives and religious fundamentalists might be more inclined to continue to support drug testing even in the face of inaccuracies. However, further analysis of these individuals (the 24% who expressed support for testing even in the face of substantial inaccuracies) revealed that there was no relationship between continued support for drug testing and political ideology or religious denomination.

There was a slight relationship between race and continued support for tests (Table 8.1). NonWhites were slightly more supportive of testing

---

[4]Other studies on the accuracy of drug-test results vary in their estimates of error. The Centers for Disease Control study results were used in this question because they provide a "worst-case" scenario. Ideally, one would want to determine the exact number of false results the public is willing to tolerate before withdrawing support. However, time constraints on the survey did not permit us to use that approach.

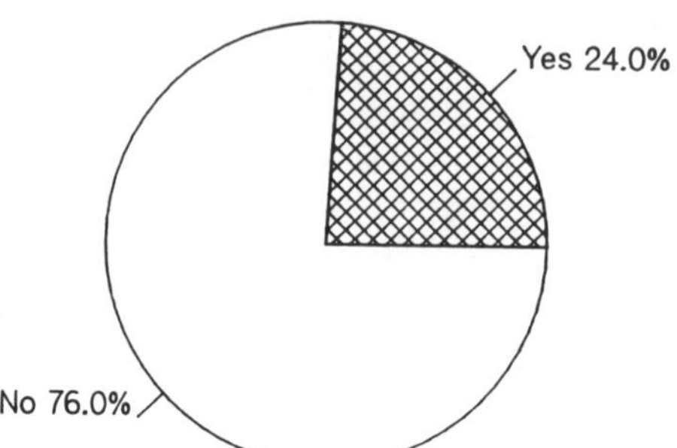

FIG. 8.4. Citizen support for drug test if as many as 6 of 10 are inaccurate ($n=684$).

than are Whites, even if such tests are inaccurate. This is remarkable in light of the potentially discriminatory effects of testing on minorities (Lindsey, 1986).

Those who are unwilling to take a drug test themselves are also unsupportive of testing others, especially in the face of inaccurate results (Table 8.2).

Balancing Individual Privacy With Public Safety

In addition to the problem of test accuracy, invasion of privacy is a key argument against drug testing by employers. Providing a specimen of bodily fluid for examination by an employer in a random testing program is tantamount to search and seizure without a warrant in the minds of some, and it may violate rules against self-incrimination. Even if there is a probable cause to suspect drug use on the job, it is probably easier to fire someone for poor performance than to require a urinalysis for illegal drugs and to risk a lawsuit (*U.S. News and World Report*, Mar. 1986). Nevertheless, a drug-testing policy can help employers screen out potential abusers during interviewing, and this may be one reason that testing has become so popular among Fortune 500 companies (*Current Accounts*, October, 1985).

TABLE 8.1
Support for Drug Testing by Respondents' Race ($N = 615$)

Would You Still Favor Testing in the Workplace if You Knew That as Many as 6 of Every 10 Tests are Wrong?	Respondents' Race	
	White	*NonWhite*
Yes	22%	34%*
No	78	66
Total	100%	100%
	$n = 529$	$n = 86$

*Significant at $p < .05$.

TABLE 8.2
Support for Drug Testing by Respondents' Willingness to Undergo Testing
Themselves (*N* = 488)

	Drug Tests are Generally Performed on Urine Samples. If You Were Asked to Take a Drug Test by Your Employer, Would You Agree to it or do You Think it Would Be an Unfair Invasion of Your Privacy?	
	Would Agree to be Tested	*Would not Agree to be Tested*
Yes	32%	21%*
No	68	79*
Total	100%	100%
	n = 315	*n* = 173

*Significant at $p < .05$.

The introduction of the privacy issue into drug testing alters support for testing. At the end of our interview, respondents were asked if they would be willing to take a drug test if asked to do so by their employers. Nearly three-fourths of respondents initially said that they would agree to the test (Fig. 8.5a). When the question was modified to indicate that it would be necessary to deliver the urine sample under the observation of a

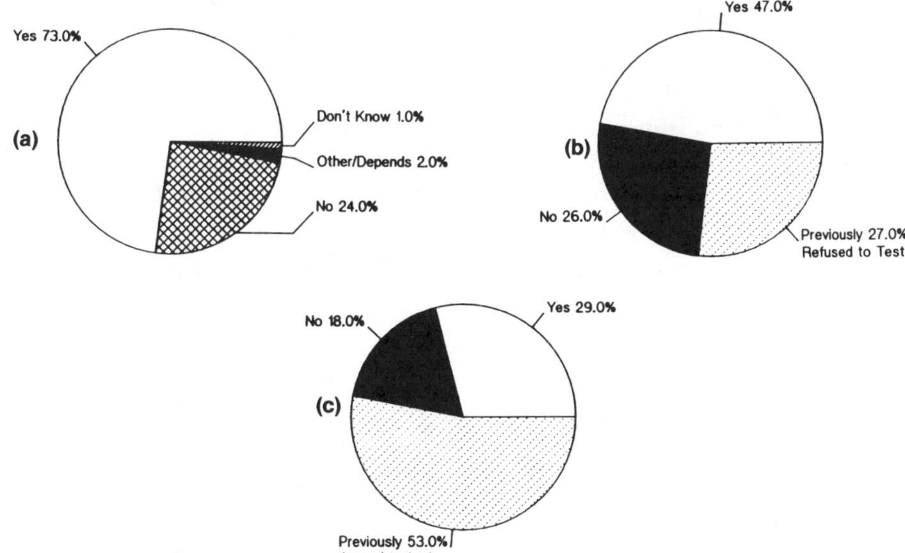

FIG. 8.5. (a) Citizen attitudes toward taking a drug test if asked by employer (*n* =700), (b) Citizen attitudes toward taking a drug test if observed (*n* =700), (c) Citizen attitudes toward taking a drug test if threatened with being fired (*n* = 700).

testing official, support for testing fell–slightly less than half of respondents said that they would take the test (Fig. 8.5b). However, when respondents were subsequently asked whether they would take an observed test if refusing meant being fired from their jobs, more than three-quarters said that they would take the test (Fig. 8.5c).

The issue of privacy appears to be of less concern to citizens than that of accuracy. Respondents who indicated support for drug testing of others tend to be willing to undergo testing themselves if asked by an employer. However, when these respondents were explicitly made aware that the urine sample must be delivered under observation, substantial numbers withdrew their willingness to undergo testing. The threat of job loss is a powerful sanction that would lead otherwise reluctant citizens to comply with observed drug tests in the workplace.

The Social Costs of Drug Testing

Putting drug-testing programs into place implies that some action will be taken based on the results. The 87% of citizens who said that they supported testing (under some circumstances) were given an opportunity to recommend a course of action for dealing with individuals whose tests yield positive results. Respondents were asked: "If a person's drug test has a positive result, do you think they should be referred to a drug counseling program, warned and then removed from their job (or team) if they test positive again, or turned in to drug law enforcement agencies?"

Figure 8.6 shows that nearly half (44%) recommended a counseling referral for those who test positive. Of the respondents, 25% advocated warning and then firing anyone who tests positive more than once, whereas 6% would turn people whose tests are positive over to law enforcement authorities.

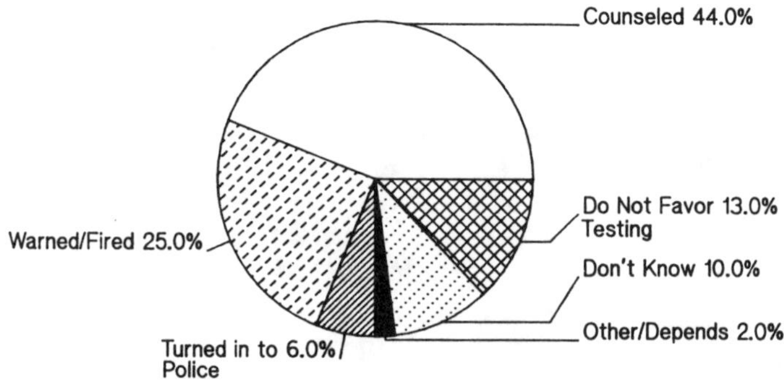

FIG. 8.6. Citizen recommendations for action if a person's drug test is positive (n =600).

Again, we looked further at those who exhibit the minority opinion. Are the 6% of respondents who would turn in their coworkers to police part of those who see drug abuse as a serious problem in their workplace? Are they disproportionately conservative? Are they any more likely to know a drug user?

Interestingly, not one of the people who advocated turning in those who test positive to police had previously indicated that drug usage is a problem in their workplaces. Only 13 of the individuals who advocated turning in to the police those people who test positive indicated that they know a marijuana user. There was no statistically significant relationship between ideology and willingness to turn those with positive tests over to the police.

DISCUSSION

In general, our study demonstrates that there is a clash of values present in attitudes toward drug testing. On the one hand, the majority of citizens support drug testing in the workplace for workers in certain job categories. On the other hand, citizens indicate that illegal drug use is not much of a problem in their own workplaces and that they have substantial doubts about the accuracy of such tests. A substantial portion of respondents withdrew their support for drug testing when told that most drug tests are inaccurate.

Although support for drug testing is demonstrated to be somewhat soft, opposition to testing is much firmer if the individual's job is not at stake. Citizens who refuse to take drug tests themselves also oppose the testing of others. Furthermore, 60% of those who initially would refuse to take a drug test continue to refuse, even if doing so means the loss of their jobs.

The questions posed to citizens in this study did not address the issue of random testing. Support that was expressed was directed at testing workers in sectors of the labor market or testing under suspicion of drug use. The outcomes of court cases based on random testing programs also suggests that random testing programs may create more problems than they solve. Screening job applicants may also prove problematic if the inaccuracy of tests proves to have discriminatory effects on hiring. The link between impaired job performance and drug use may also be a critical factor in gaining general acceptance of drug-testing programs.

Public concern about the accuracy of tests appears to outweigh privacy concerns, in the abstract worst-case scenario. Of course, citizens still may tolerate low levels of test inaccuracy. When confronted with the prospect of urinating while being viewed by another person, the salience of the privacy issue may change for many people. In terms of policy, it would be prudent to define rather narrowly and specifically the conditions under which testing may be conducted, including testing for alcohol and other legal substances that can impair job performance. Procedures for protecting the individual's privacy and for guaranteeing the accuracy of tests should be defined simultaneously, and the actions taken with respect to individuals who test positive must be clearly stated and agreed to by each worker prior to testing.

REFERENCES

Braden, W. (1986, September 28). Politically, Illinois is a scaled-down U.S. *Chicago Sun-Times,* p. 13.

Brelis, M. & Schneider, A. (1986a, October 19). Pilot with heart damage ok'd to fly, died with businessman in copter crash. *The Pittsburgh Press,* pp. A1, A14.

Brelis, M. & Schneider, A. (1986b, November 30). Hooked pilots trapped between cocaine, grounding. *The Pittsburgh Press,* pp. A1, A14.

Campbell, A. (1978). *The sense of well being in America.* New York: McGraw-Hill.

CBS/New York Times Poll. (1986). *Drugs in America.* Released September 1 (Press release).

Gest, T. (1985, December 23). Using drugs? You may not get hired. *U.S. News & World Report,* p. 38.

Glantz, L. H. (1986, October 4). Employers should not be law enforcers. *New York Times,* p. 12.

Johnston, L., O'Malley, P. M., & Bachman, G. G. (1986, July 7). Drug use among American high school students and other young adults. (National trends through 1985.) News release from the National Institute on Drug Abuse, Washington, DC.

Kerr, P. (1986, December 11). Drug tests losing most court cases: Suits force a halt in 13 of 17 suits against the government. *New York Times,* p. 5.

Lindsey, R. (1986, May 3). Worker drug test provoking debate. *New York Times,* p. 3.

Safire, W. (1986, August 11). Prove yourself innocent. *New York Times.* p. 8.

Schneider, A. (1986a, September 21). Pilots on drugs – Doctors can't report them. *The Pittsburgh Press,* pp. A1, A4.

Schneider, A. (1986b, September 24). Doctors, pilots back law to report drug users. *The Pittsburgh Press,* pp. A1, A6.

Schneider, A. (1986c, December 4). Secret treatment of addicted pilots a dangerous practice. *The Pittsburgh Press,* pp. A1, A6.

Schneider, A. (1986d, December 4). Cocaine treatment must recognize social pressure. *The Pittsburgh Press.* pp. A1, A4.

Schneider, A. (1986e, December 21). Air crews fly through customs because they're called low risk. *The Pittsburgh Press,* pp. A1, A11.

Schneider, A. (1986f, December 21). Lax air-crew checks open drug door. *The Pittsburgh Press,* pp. A1, A10.

Schneider, A., & Bowman, L. (1986, Ocbtober 12). Forbidden to drive for drinking, pilots still in skies. *The Pittsburgh Press.* pp. A1, A20.

Schneider, A., & Brelis, M. (1986a, October 12). Pilot physicals inadequate, doctors charge. *The Pittsburgh Press.* pp. A1, A4.

Schneider, A., & Brelis, M. (1986, October 19). Anatomy of a system that didn't work. *The Pittsburgh Press,* pp. A1, A20.

A test tube war on drugs. (1986, March 17) *U.S. News and World Report,* p. 27.

Thornton, M. (1986, June 26). Drug tests called costly, often useless. *The Washington Post,* pp. 1–13.

Worker drug tests spread despite deep controversy. (1985, October). *Current Accounts,* p. 13.

9

America's Drug Problem in the Media: Is It Real or Is It Memorex?

Lloyd D. Johnston
University of Michigan

Earlier chapters have established that a plethora of stories about drugs appeared in the U.S. media during 1986. The alarm was sounded. The public, members of Congress, and the Administration all took up arms to renew America's war on drugs – culminating in the Omnibus Drug Bill being passed by the Congress and signed by President Reagan in late 1986.

But was this alarm in sync with actual drug abuse in the country? Some in the media have been quite vocal in saying that it was *out* of sync; examples include reporter Adam Weisman's (1986) *New Republic* article, "I was a drug-hype junkie," and Diamond, Accosta, and Thornton's (1987) *TV Guide* article, "Is TV news hyping America's cocaine problem?". They charge that the media "hyped" the drug story – that all of the media attention came well after the problem had peaked. As it happens, both of the articles just cited relied heavily on the data from this study to make their points.

But are the media guilty of hyping the drug story? I propose to examine this issue primarily by using data from an ongoing series of national surveys of adolescents and young adults entitled "Monitoring the Future."

This ongoing study is one that I and my colleagues, Jerald Bachman and Patrick O'Malley, have been conducting since 1975 through the University of Michigan's Institute for Social Research. Using large, nationally representative samples of high school seniors ($N=17,000$ per year) from every graduating class since 1975, we have tracked the size and nature of the drug epidemic among America's high school students. Using data from annual follow-ups of representative subsamples from all of these past graduating classes ($N=1,000$ per year per class), we have been able to do much the same in recent years for American college students and for young adults who are high school graduates (see Johnston, O'Malley, & Bachman, 1987). All of these data have been provided to the national media on a fairly timely basis by both the project and the sponsoring agency (the National Institute on Drug Abuse) and have received widespread media coverage nationwide over the years.

The observations in this chapter are derived not only from the results of the study itself, however, but also from our many experiences with the media as a result of disseminating the study's findings. That is, our conclusions of how the mass media have covered the drug issue are based in part on our observations as participant–observers. In the course of our issuing one or two national press releases each year for the past several years, we have talked with reporters from virtually all of the nation's media. In addition, as the drug issue heated up in 1986, I participated in some 200 to 300 press interviews and gained almost an insider's view of how reporters, if not publishers, were thinking during the historical period in question.

CONCERNS AMONG THOSE IN THE MEDIA

Was the drug crisis portrayed by the media in 1986 a reflection of a current problem, or was it simply a much-delayed picture of a crisis that had already peaked and declined? As a participant–observer of how the drug story developed in 1986, I can verify that this question was very much on the minds of many reporters, and it grew more troublesome for them as the drug story crescendoed and culminated in what can at best be described as hastily drafted Federal legislation. (There were also other excesses at the height of this frenzy: Congressional candidates challenged each other to prove the purity of their excretions, if not their thoughts, in what came to be known as "jar wars.")

After the Omnibus Drug Bill was signed into law, after the Congressional elections were over, and after a few reporters chastised their colleagues by claiming that this all was due to a bad case of media hype, there emerged an almost eerie silence in the media on the subject of drugs. Guilt and withdrawal for self-assessment among those in the media explains a lot of this "refractory period."

Were those in the media justified in feeling guilty? Only partly so, if you accept my answer to the question, "Is it real or is it Memorex?" I would argue that to a certain degree it is both. In some ways, the sense of a crisis concerning drugs came well after a turnaround had occurred in

America's drug epidemic, broadly defined. But, if you take into account the mercurial nature of "the drug problem," which has resulted from constant qualitative shifts in the epidemic, then the sense of alarm communicated by the media and expressed by the public was right on target.

THE EVIDENCE FOR "MEMOREX"

The U.S. drug problem peaked much earlier than 1986, the year when media coverage of drugs peaked. I rely heavily on the national data from our own studies to support this statement, although there are other good survey sources to substantiate the point (National Institute on Drug Abuse, 1983, 1987a). Figure 9.1 shows that the percentage of high school seniors who had at least tried an illicit drug peaked in 1981. Figure 9.2 shows that the *active* use of illicit drugs—defined as any use in the prior month—was at its highest in 1978.

The shaded areas of the bars in Fig. 9.2 show the proportion of seniors who reported using an illicit drug *other* than marijuana during the prior month. Although use of illicit drugs other than marijuana peaked later than the active use of all illicit drugs (in 1981 instead of in 1978), this is still 5 years prior to the peak in media and public attention achieved in 1986.

Perhaps even more importantly, over the 5-year period between 1981 and 1986, both of these measures of active drug use among high school seniors reveal steady declines; our data for young adults show much the same trends. Clearly, the peak in involvement with illicit drugs by American young people occurred some 5 or more years prior to the public frenzy of 1986.

Much of the down turn in drug use by young Americans can be attributed to a decline in the use of marijuana, the drug that received much of the public's concern and attention in the late 1970s and early 1980s. But the use of other drugs has also been declining, including the use of sedatives, tranquilizers, hallucinogens, and (more recently) amphetamines, as Table 9.1 documents. So why wasn't the peak media attention achieved until 1986?

One explanation involves the mercurial nature of the drug epidemic. In the early 1970s heroin was of the greatest concern, until LSD took the spotlight, largely because of its growing popularity in combination with its alleged dangers. Then PCP came along, and, although it captured center stage for a short while, it faded rapidly in popularity—largely, in my opinion, because it gained a well-deserved reputation on the street as a very harmful drug.

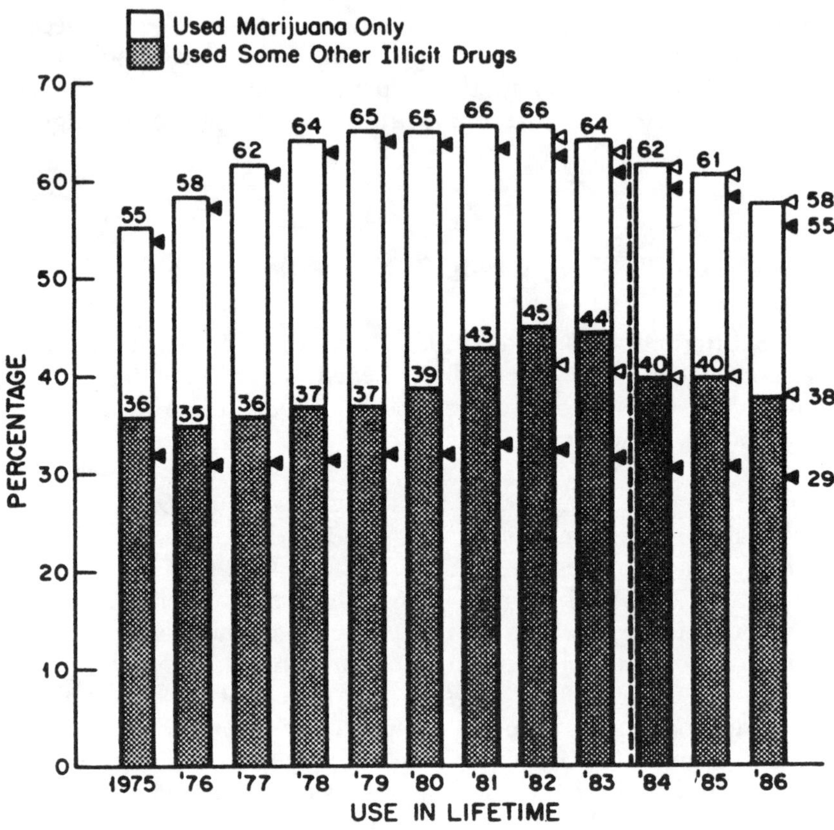

FIG. 9.1. Trends in lifetime prevalence of an illicit drug-use index—High School seniors (source: Johnston et al., 1987).
NOTES: Use of "some other illicit drugs" includes any use of hallucinogens, cocaine, and heroin, or any use that is not under a doctor's orders of other opiates, stimulants, sedatives, or tranquilizers.
◄ indicates the percentage that results if all stimulants are excluded from the definition of "illicit drugs." < shows the percentage that results if only nonprescription stimulants are excluded.
The dashed vertical line indicates that after 1983 the shaded and open bars are defined by using the amphetamine questions that were revised to exclude nonprescription stimulants from the definition of "illicit drugs."

Marijuana was also of concern throughout the 1970s, but it was the growing number of heavy marijuana users in the mid-1970s that shifted the focus more onto marijuana. However, as the health message got through, the frequency of daily use dropped dramatically between 1978 and 1986 (see Johnston et al., 1987) and was followed by a drop in public and media concern with marijuana. In essence, society had been partially successful in its efforts to control the use of this drug.

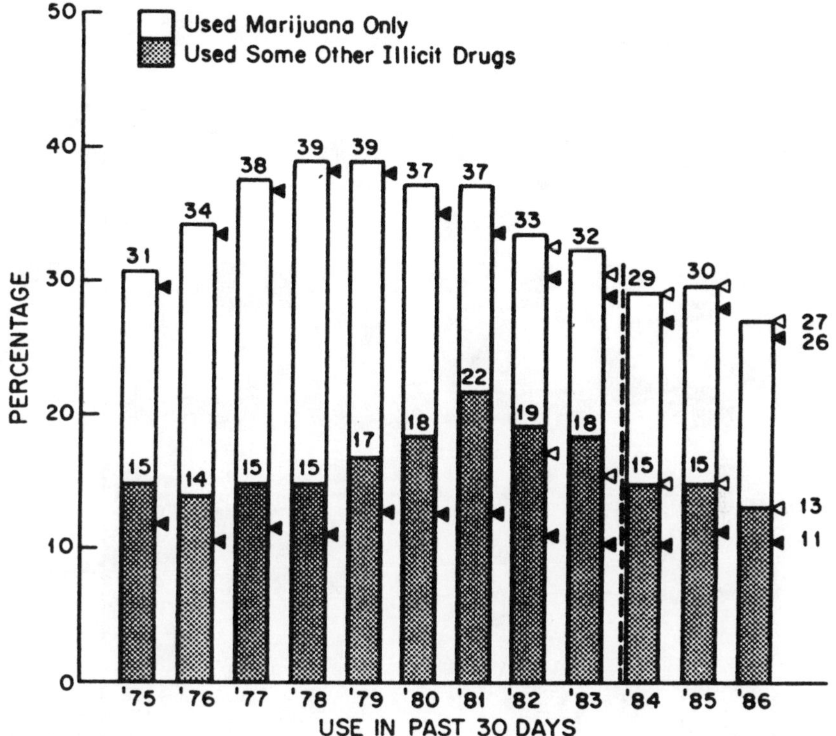

FIG. 9.2. Trends in 30-day prevalence of an illicit drug-use index–High School seniors (source: Johnston et al., 1987).
NOTES: Use of "some other illicit drugs" includes any use of hallucinogens, cocaine, and heroin, or any use that is not under a doctor's orders of other opiates, stimulants, sedatives, or tranquilizers.
◄ indicates the percentage that results if all stimulants are excluded from the definition of "illicit drugs." < shows the percentage that results if only non-prescription stimulants are excluded.
The dashed vertical line indicates that after 1983 the shaded and open bars are defined by using the amphetamine questions that were revised to exclude nonprescription stimulants from the definition of "illicit drugs."

THE EVIDENCE FOR A REAL CRISIS IN 1986

Cocaine was the last drug to enter center stage. As Fig. 9.3 and 9.4 illustrate, the overall prevalence of cocaine use among American adolescents and young adults rose sharply in the late 1970s and then leveled off around 1980 (Johnston et al., 1987; National Institute on Drug Abuse, 1987a). Cocaine use then remained high, but level, between 1980 and 1986.

However, to say that it remained level is deceptively reassuring in two ways. First, cocaine use remained at peak levels during those years despite

TABLE 9.1
Trends in Annual Prevalence of 17 Types of Drugs

Percent Who Used in Last 12 Months

Approx. N =	Class of 1975 (9,400)	Class of 1976 (15,400)	Class of 1977 (17,100)	Class of 1978 (17,800)	Class of 1979 (15,500)	Class of 1980 (15,900)	Class of 1981 (17,500)	Class of 1982 (17,700)	Class of 1983 (16,300)	Class of 1984 (15,900)	Class of 1985 (16,000)	Class of 1986 (15,200)	'85–'86 Change
Marijuana/Hashish	40.0	44.5	47.6	50.2	50.8	48.8	46.1	44.3	42.3	40.0	40.6	38.8	−1.8
Inhalants[a]	NA	3.0	3.7	4.1	5.4	4.6	4.1	4.5	4.3	5.1	5.7	6.1	+0.4
Inhalants Adjusted[b]	*NA*	*NA*	*NA*	*NA*	*8.9*	*7.9*	*6.1*	*6.6*	*6.2*	*7.2*	*7.5*	*8.9*	*+1.4s*
Amyl & Butyl Nitrites[c]	NA	NA	NA	NA	6.5	5.7	3.7	3.6	3.6	4.0	4.0	4.7	+0.7
Hallucinogens	11.2	9.4	8.8	9.6	9.9	9.3	9.0	8.1	7.3	6.5	6.3	6.0	−0.3
Hallucinogens Adjusted[d]	*NA*	*NA*	*NA*	*NA*	*11.8*	*10.4*	*10.1*	*9.0*	*8.3*	*7.3*	*7.6*	*7.6*	*0.0*
LSD	7.2	6.4	5.5	6.3	6.6	6.5	6.5	6.1	5.4	4.7	4.4	4.5	+0.1
PCP[c]	NA	NA	NA	NA	7.0	4.4	3.2	2.2	2.6	2.3	2.9	2.4	−0.5
Cocaine	5.6	6.0	7.2	9.0	12.0	12.3	12.4	11.5	11.4	11.6	13.1	12.7	−0.4
"Crack"[c]	NA	NA	NA	NA	NA	NA	NA	NA	NA	NA	NA	4.1	NA
Heroin	1.0	0.8	0.8	0.8	0.5	0.5	0.5	0.6	0.6	0.5	0.6	0.5	−0.1
Other opiates[e]	5.7	5.7	6.4	6.0	6.2	6.3	5.9	5.3	5.1	5.2	5.9	5.2	−0.7s
Stimulants[e]	16.2	15.8	16.3	17.1	18.3	20.8	26.0	26.1	24.6	NA	NA	NA	NA
Stimulants Adjusted[c,f]	*NA*	*NA*	*NA*	*NA*	*NA*	*NA*	*NA*	*20.3*	*17.9*	*17.7*	*15.8*	*13.4*	*−2.4sss*
Sedatives[e]	11.7	10.7	10.8	9.9	9.9	10.3	10.5	9.1	7.9	6.6	5.8	5.2	−0.6
Barbiturates[e]	10.7	9.6	9.3	8.1	7.5	6.8	6.6	5.5	5.2	4.9	4.6	4.2	−0.4
Metaqualone[e]	5.1	4.7	5.2	4.9	5.9	7.2	7.6	6.8	5.4	3.8	2.8	2.1	−0.7s
Tranquilizers[e]	10.6	10.3	10.8	9.9	9.6	8.7	8.0	7.0	6.9	6.1	6.1	5.8	−0.3
Alcohol	84.8	85.7	87.0	87.7	88.1	87.9	87.0	86.8	87.3	86.0	85.6	84.4	−1.1
Cigarettes	NA	NA	NA	NA	NA	NA	NA	NA	NA	NA	NA	NA	NA

Notes: Level of significance of difference between the two most recent classes: $s = .05$, $ss = .01$, $sss = .001$. NA indicates data not available.

[a]Data based on four questionnaire forms. N is four-fifths of N indicated.

[b]Adjusted for underreporting of amyl and buyl nitrites. See text for details.

[c]Data based on a single questionnaire form. N is one-fifth of N indicated.

[d]Adjusted for underreporting of PCP. See text for details.

[e]Only drug use that was not under a doctor's orders is included here.

[f]Based on the data from the revised question, which attempts to exclude the inappropriate reporting of nonprescription stimulants.

Source: Johnston et al. (1987).

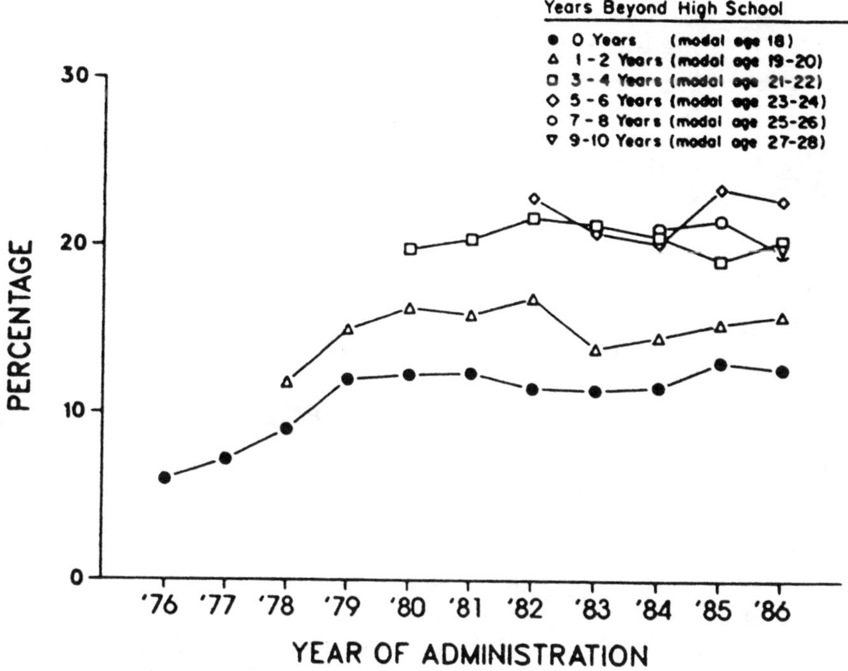

FIG. 9.3. Cocaine: Trends in annual prevalence among young adults by age group (source: Johnston et al., 1987).

dramatic efforts on the part of the government to win its "war on drugs" – a war that was largely aimed at cocaine use. Second, although the number of active cocaine users among adolescents and young adults did not increase much during the 1980s, the forms of their use became more dangerous and the casualties from use skyrocketed.

The lack of success of the "war on drugs" may be the least recognized contributor to the dramatic increase in public concern about drugs in 1986. As was widely reported in the 1980s, the Federal government substantially increased its efforts to close the supply of drugs (particularly cocaine) at the U.S. borders. Drug enforcement activities inside the country also continued to increase and, because of their graphic quality, got particular attention in the electronic media. Television coverage made the raids familiar: a battering ram for the door; the heavily armed police; the drugs, money, and guns that were confiscated; and the handcuffed suspects being led away. Yet, despite all of this action and the expenditure of billions of dollars on enforcement, there was constant evidence that we were losing the war on drugs. Something was wrong. The public and the media both knew it, and both were increasingly frustrated and alarmed at the inability of their social institutions to handle the problem.

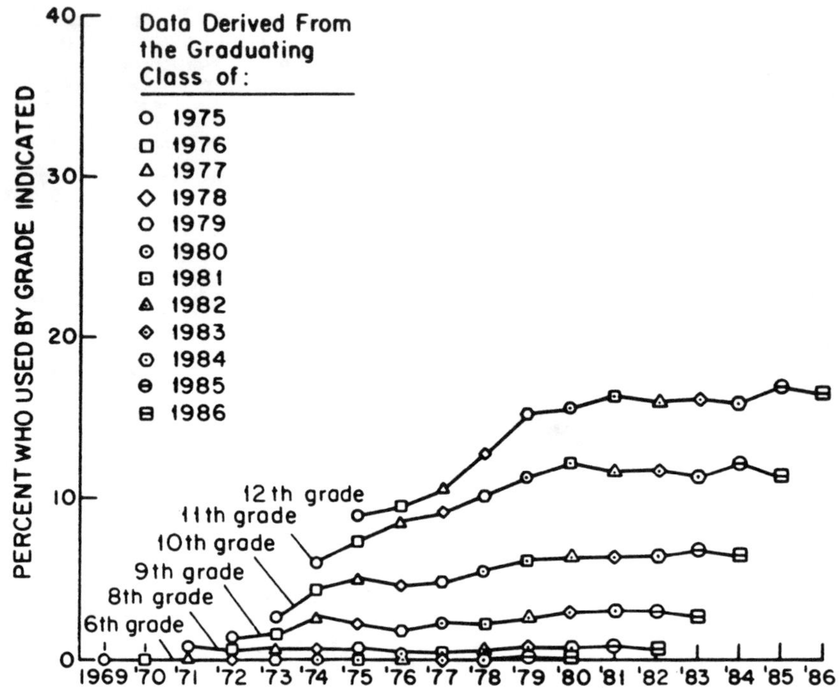

FIG. 9.4. Cocaine: Trends in lifetime prevalence for earlier grade levels (based on retrospective reports from seniors; source: Johnston et al., 1987).

Evidence that we were losing the drug war came in part from law enforcement officers themselves. On many occasions they pointed out that they were seizing only about 10% of the drugs imported into this country and that they were overwhelmed by the resources and sophistication of the drug smugglers and by the need to secure thousands of miles of national borders (*Newsweek,* 1985; *USA Today,* 1987; *U.S. News and World Report,* 1984). The public surely was alarmed by the brazenness of the drug smugglers and dealers—from their repeated assassinations of government officials in Colombia, to their buying off of judges and law enforcement officials all along the way, to their openly selling crack to youngsters on the street corners of America's cities.

Lest there be any question that the availability of drugs was increasing while the U.S. government struggled even harder to stem the tide, Drug Enforcement Administration (DEA) figures on the price and purity of cocaine tell a vivid story. These measures are taken as indicators of the availability of cocaine, on the assumption that increasing purity and decreasing cost both indicate greater availability. Based on undercover street buys, the DEA estimated that the average purity of cocaine, sold at retail, rose from about 33% in 1982 to about 60% in 1986; the average wholesale price of a kilogram of cocaine dropped fairly steadily, from about $60,000 in 1982 to about $35,000 in 1986. (These figures are based on midpoints of the range given for each year. See Drug Enforcement Administration and Royal Canadian Mounted Police, 1987.)

The American public was generally aware that the flood of cocaine was not being stemmed – although it may not have been aware of these specific figures – and this awareness gave rise to a sense of alarm, fear, and anger.

CONTINUING INCREASES IN CASUALTIES

There was also other evidence that we were losing the war on drugs. Despite the leveling of the overall prevalence of drug use, the statistics on the "casualties" of cocaine were, and still are, rising dramatically. Accord-

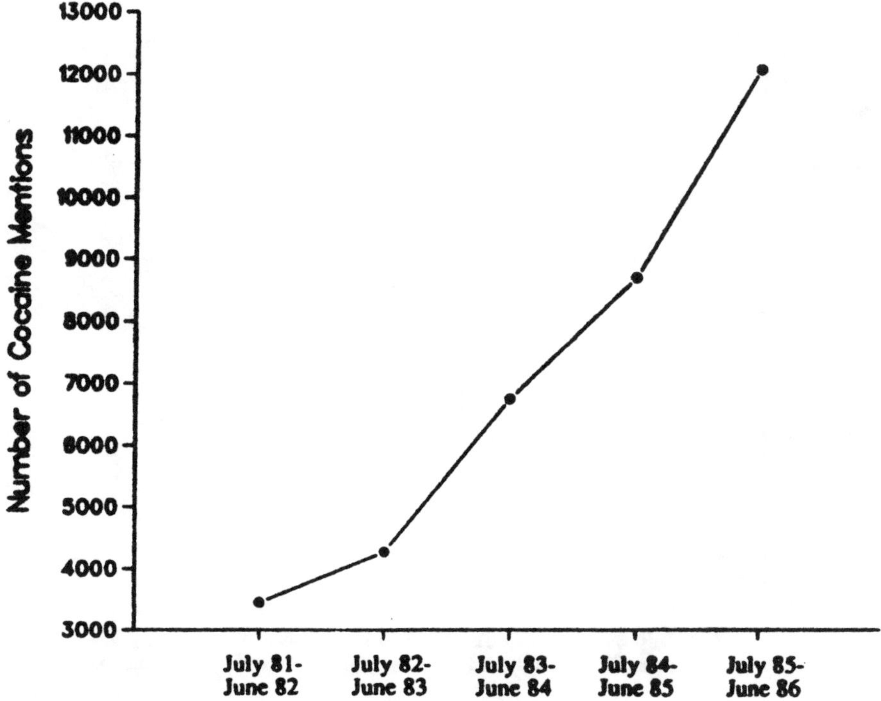

FIG. 9.5. Trends in number of mentions of cocaine in emergency room episodes. (Excludes emergency rooms that did not meet the consistently reporting facility selection criteria. Numbers of emergency room mentions include data imputed for gaps in reporting. Also excludes Newark. Source: National Institute on Drug Abuse, Drug Abuse Warning Network, unpublished data.)

ing to data from the National Institute on Drug Abuse's DAWN system—the Drug Abuse Warning Network (National Institute on Drug Abuse, 1987b)—a large, nationwide panel of hospital emergency rooms showed a nearly 300% increase in medical emergencies related to cocaine between 1982 and 1986 (from 3,469 medical emergencies between July 1981 and June 1982 to 12,104 between July 1985 and June 1986). Figure 9.5 charts this trend. The 12,000 mentions in 1986 reflect a drug-related emergency rate that is about 40% higher than just one year later.

Figure 9.6 shows another series of statistics from the same DAWN system, this one based on coroners' reports of deaths in which cocaine was present. It shows about a 250% increase in cocaine-related deaths over the same 4-year interval, with the increase continuing into 1986. Although empirical evidence on treatment programs is more sparse, there also appears to have been a great increase in treatment demand for cocaine addiction over the same interval.

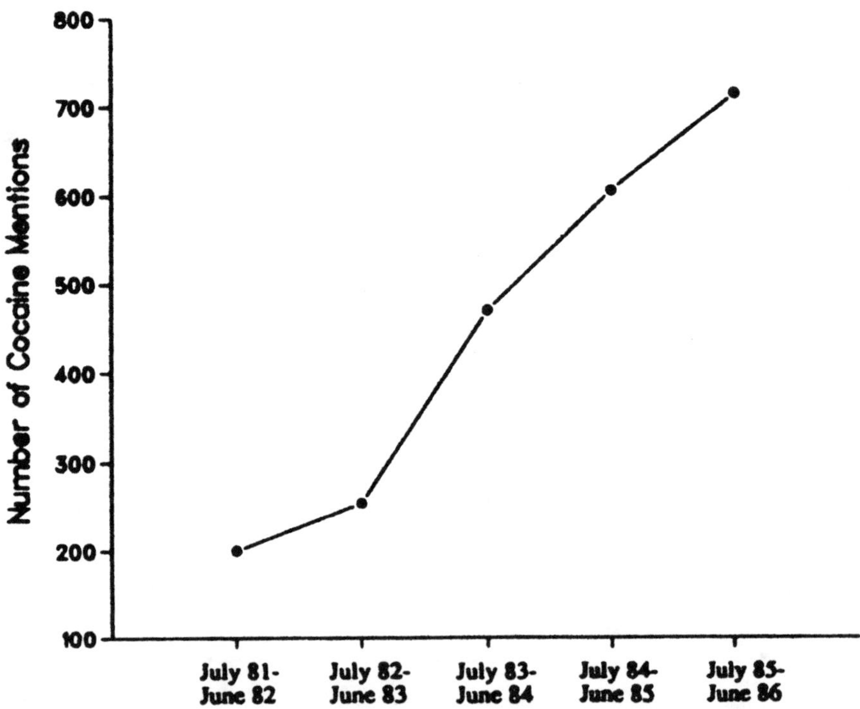

FIG. 9.6. Trends in number of mentions of cocaine in drug-abuse related deaths. (Medical examiner data from New York are not included in this table because of incomplete reporting. Also excludes Newark. Source: NIDA, Drug Abuse Warning Network, unpublished data.)

These dramatic increases in cocaine casualties are, in my opinion, the result of at least three factors. First, the increased rate of cocaine initiation in the late 1970s was bearing its bitter fruit 4 to 6 years later, after the rather long "honeymoon period" often observed for cocaine snorters is over and some portion of them become addicted. Second, the increased purity of the available cocaine may well have led to a higher conversion rate into addiction and/or a higher rate of overdose reactions among users. The third reason for the increase in casualties was the growing popularity of more dangerous forms of ingestion, probably due to there having emerged a larger pool or experienced users in the population who might be willing to "move up" to a riskier but higher high, but also certainly due to the introduction of crack—a very cheap and very easy-to-use form of freebase.

Data from the ongoing study of high school seniors help substantiate these interpretations. Figure 9.7 shows the proportion of all seniors in each year who say they have both used cocaine at least once in the prior year and had some experience smoking it (crack is smoked). Note the sharp rise between 1983 and 1986, from roughtly 2.5% to more than 6%

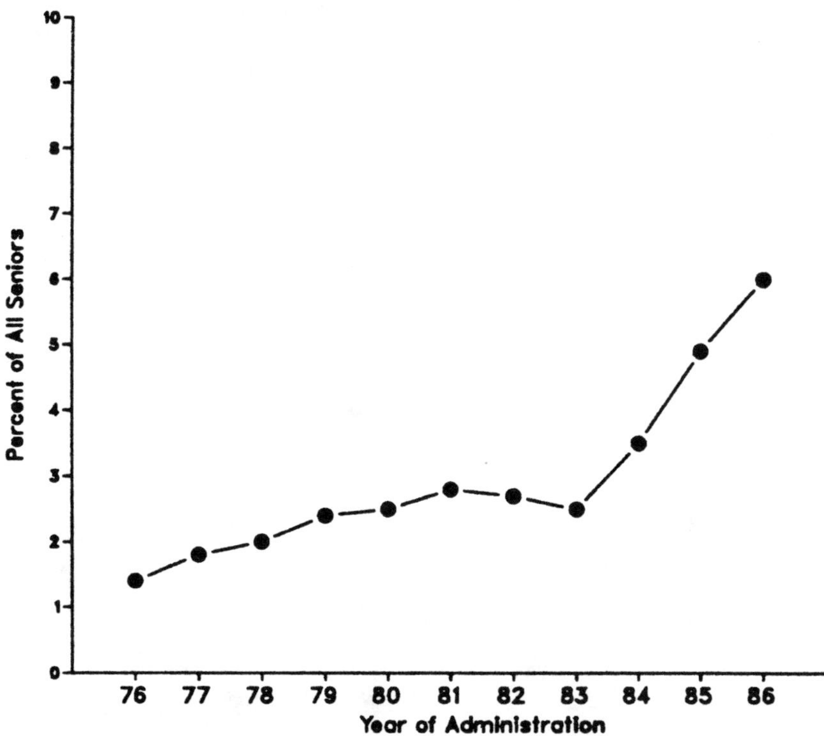

FIG. 9.7. Trends in percent of all seniors who are past-year cocaine users and have *smoked* cocaine (source: Monitoring the Future study).

of all American high school seniors, and this does not even include the drop-out segment. Certainly a more dangerous form of ingestion (smoking) was evolving, no doubt due in large part to the increased use of crack.

Figure 9.8 shows the proportion of seniors who said they had used cocaine 20 or more times in the past 30 days. Although the absolute percentages are low, note that there was a doubling between 1984 and 1986 in daily or near-daily use. Although this is not a measure of addiction per se, such frequent use has to be highly correlated with addiction.

Finally, Fig. 9.9 presents trends in the proportion of seniors who say that they have used some cocaine in the prior year and that they had tried to quit and could not. This second indicator of addiction also shows a considerable increase since 1978, but particularly increased after 1984 when crack came onto the scene.

Obviously an increasing number of young Americans were getting into trouble with cocaine. Further, the number who were exposing themselves to these dangers is stunning. Although "only" about 17% of seniors in recent high school classes—or about 1 in 6—reported any experience with cocaine before leaving high school, 40% of previous graduating classes reported trying cocaine by age 27– 4 in every 10.

It is fair to say that we did have a drug crisis in 1986, once you take into account (a) the addictive potential of cocaine, (b) the increasingly danger-

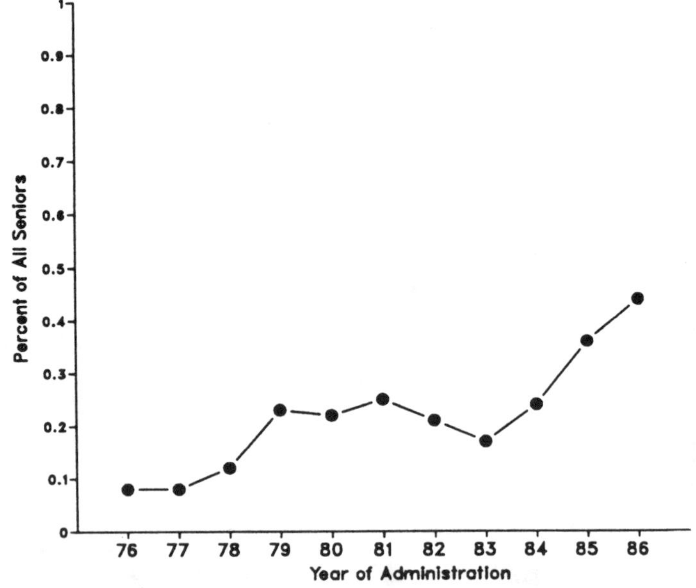

FIG. 9.8. Trends in percent of seniors who used cocaine daily in the past 30 days (source: Monitoring the Future study).

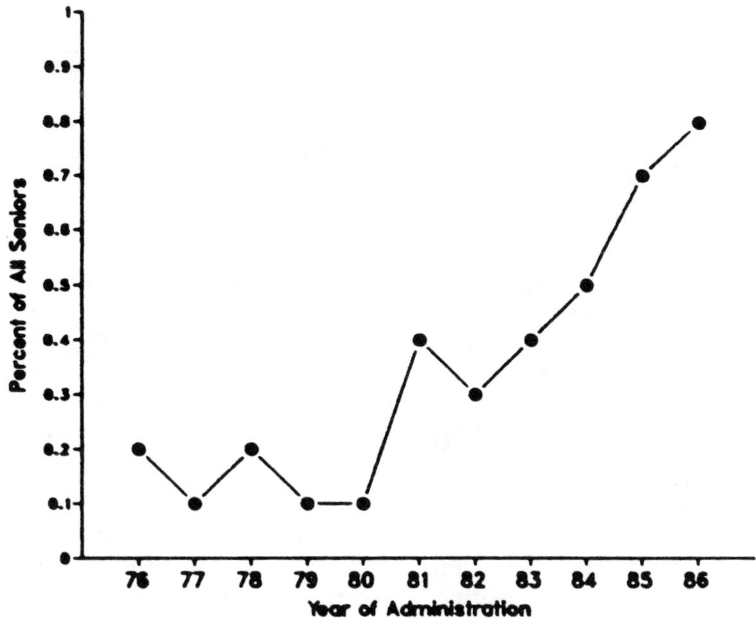

FIG. 9.9. Trends in percent of seniors who tried to stop using cocaine and failed (source: Monitoring the Future study).

ous forms in which it was being used, (c) the rapidly increasing rate of casualties that were occurring, (d) the increasing availability and dropping prices (which made crack, in particular, accessible to younger age groups), and (e) the degree of penetration of cocaine use into the youthful population. It was admittedly a qualitatively different drug crisis than the one that existed in 1980. Fewer people used illicit drugs in 1986 than in 1980 – marijuana use had especially declined, and use of amphetamines and barbiturates was also down – but more people were at risk of addiction and overdose reactions because of what they were using and how they were using it.

CONCLUSIONS

Certainly there were excesses in the media coverage of the drug problem in 1986, both in local and national reporting. In fact, one of the most vivid examples of exploitive television I can remember was the 1986 Geraldo Rivera 2-hour special on the drug crisis, "American Vice: The Doping of a Nation." Ironically, Rivera had the storyline right – this country's attempts to close down the drug supply are doomed to failure and the real answer lies in dealing with the demand–education side of the equation. However, he took the media's obsession with the visual drama of drug busts to its highest form, by giving the viewer live drug raids – doors were hammered in; people (including possibly innocent ones) were arrested on camera; drugs, guns, and money were placed on display. Despite Rivera's own conclusion about the importance of demand reduction, however, most people's memories of this program will center on the supply reduction efforts – the drug busts. These are a lot more graphic, dramatic, and colorful than pictures of kids in prevention classes, parents working together, and city councils discussing new policies – the visuals that might be associated with demand reduction.

If I were to fault the media for their impact on the drug problem, it would not be for hyping the problem. There was a real crisis, and some constructive results followed that attention, including more (although still limited) federal funding for demand–reduction strategies; a more widespread public awareness of the dangers of crack, which probably helped contain its spread; and a galvanizing of public commitment to do something about "the drug problem," within both the private and public sectors. These are all positive outcomes, some of which were long overdue.

My criticisms of the media focus primarily on television and on the way in which it put visual drama above substance. This emphasis on the visual clearly hyped one type of solution. Television showed an endless chain of drug busts and airplane and boat chases, almost to the exclusion of a more thoughtful and penetrating consideration of other possible solutions. Prevention and demand–reduction strategies generally are getting increasing lip service paid to them today in news coverage and in Congressional debates; but when you look at where the column inches, program minutes, and federal dollars go, only a very small portion goes to demand reduction. So it is here, in the area of policy responses, that I would like to see the electronic media consciously work against Marshall McLuhan's maxim – to try to prevent the medium from being the message. The resulting inability of our society to deal effectively with such a serious problem among our young people is too high a price to pay for entertainment in the news.

REFERENCES

Banks, drugs, terrorists – FBI picks its targets. (1985, April 22). *U.S. News and World Report,* pp. 63–64.

Diamond, E., Accosta, F., & Thornton, L. J. (1987, February 7). Is TV news hyping America's cocaine problem? *TV Guide,* pp. 4–10.

Drug Enforcement Administration and the Royal Canadian Mounted Police. (1987). *The illicit drug situation in the United States and Canada*. Washington, DC: U.S. Government Printing Office (Publ. No. 1987-177-413-814/60358).

Drug war termed "sad state of affairs." (1987, March 19). *USA Today*, p. 40.

A G-man's anger. (1985, March 18). *Newsweek*, p. 30.

Johnston, L.D., O'Malley, P.M., & Bachman, J.G. (1987). *National trends in drug use and related factors among American high school students and young adults, 1975–1986*. Washington, DC: National Institute on Drug Abuse: DHHS Publ. No. (ADM) 87-1535.

National Institute on Drug Abuse (1983). *National survey on drug abuse: Main findings, 1982*. Washington, DC: DHHS Publ. No. (ADM) 83-1262.

National Institute on Drug Abuse (1987a). *National household survey on drug abuse: Population estimates, 1985*. Washington, DC: DHHS Publ. No. (ADM) 87-1539.

National Institute on Drug Abuse (1987b). *Data from the Drug Abuse Warning Network: Semiannual report, trend data through July-December 1986* (NIDA Statistical Series G, No. 19). Washington, DC: DHHS Publ. No. (ADM) 87-1529.

Weisman, A. P. (1986, October 6). 48 hours on crack street: I was a drug-hype junkie. *The New Republic*, pp. 14–17.

10

Dealing with Illicit Drugs: The Power—and Limits— of Mass Media Agenda Setting

Donald L. Shaw
University of North Carolina at Chapel Hill

Maxwell E. McCombs
University of Texas at Austin

America has a drug problem. In 1988 some presidential candidates were urging a war on drugs. In 1986 there were 24,847 visits to emergency rooms related to cocaine overdose, a 245% increase over the year 1983. Comparing the same 2 years, the increase in emergency room visits for heroin or morphine was only 23% and marijuana, 8%. Emergency room visits for alcohol dropped by 15% in the same period (*U.S. News and World Report,* March 21, 1988, p. 73).

Chapter 2 detailed three on-going data collection programs of the National Institute on Drug Abuse to measure trends in drug usage among Americans, especially the younger Americans who soon will control our government, businesses, schools, and military. There is ample evidence in these measures that drugs occupy a prominent position on the personal, behavioral agenda of a significant number of Americans. Unfortunately, drugs are at or near the top of the agenda for a sizeable minority. America has a drug problem.

THE MEDIA WORLD

In recent years this drug problem has been prominent on the agenda of our news media. There has been extensive coverage of drugs on the nightly news, in documentaries, and on the pages of our daily newspapers. But media coverage of drug abuse has not paralleled the behavioral agenda. Tracking this coverage across the past 5 years, chapter 4 documented a very uneven pattern. Although the media agenda is not created from whole cloth, it nevertheless infrequently parallels broad social trends.

113

Media coverage, as noted in chapter 9, is a mixture of real-world events and trends filtered through the professional traditions and values of journalism.

News is not just factual information. It is an act of creative construction, influenced and guided by professional standards. Choices are made about stories; headlines are written; space is allocated. Reporters and editors do not consciously "construct an agenda." They report news. Yet, these journalistic choices often frame the way we see the world because there is so much happening that we cannot individually see it all, regardless of how far and often we travel or the number of people to whom we talk. We have to live part of our lives, if we are to be good citizens, in what Walter Lippmann (1922) called a "pseudo environment." It nevertheless is the environment in which we have to decide on how to allocate taxes between social programs versus the military, to raise or lower taxes, and to decide if the country will be led by Democrats or Republicans.

Lippmann's analysis of public opinion also made clear that there is a kind of social Darwinism of public issues. Issues have to compete for space in our pseudo environment. Research has suggested that the public at most can think about only five to seven public issues at any one time (Miller, 1956), and most individuals can list only about two to three when public opinion pollsters ask. Many list just one. Some can name no public issues at all.

Lippmann argued that a "new" issue rises at the expense of an "old" one. We cannot consider and deal with an infinite number at once. In the 1920s, Lippmann cited the rise of public concern over the infant death rate (a concern of Americans again today), but pointed out that until the press took up the issue, "voters and municipal officials did not have a place in their environment for those babies" (Lippmann, 1922, p. 30).

When a cue ball strikes the end of a contiguous row of other billiard balls, it stops and another billiard ball flies off the far end of the row. In a similar—but far less dramatic—fashion, news, and news events sometimes alter the press and public agenda. As the press discovered the issue of child health, so did voters and officials. Recent news media attention to serious American illicit drug usage is producing the same result (Beniger, 1978).

Across the past 15 years, as chapter 7 documented, public concern about drugs has followed the ebb and flow of media coverage. Increases in news coverage resulted in increased nominations of drugs as the most important problem facing this country. Decreased coverage resulted in fewer mentions of drugs. This is the heart of the agenda-setting phenomenon documented by two decades of empirical research: The issues on the media agenda influence the salience of issues on the public agenda. Although the media seldom determine our attitudes and opinions and tell us what to think, they frequently tell us what to think about (Cohen, 1963). In other words, the media can set the public agenda (McCombs & Shaw, 1972).

It is important to map the media agenda and the public agenda, both the agenda of personal concerns and the behavioral agenda. Knowledge of these trends is important and useful. But if we want to ameliorate the problem of drugs and to influence these trends, knowledge of the dynamics of agenda building is essential. The evidence in chapter 7 on the agenda-setting role of the press is extremely useful in this regard. It demonstrates that the news media can get the public's attention. Furthermore, this attention and concern can be rallied in a relatively short time, a matter of months, not years or decades. Despite their imperfections and limitations, the news media do play the role assigned them by democratic theory. They alert and inform the public about significant social issues.

SPOTLIGHTING ISSUES

News changes constantly, as events occur. From this collage of events, issues arise that are not so transitory. Events are the soil from which issues grow, so that if the news media, for example, focus heavily on crime stories, then the issue of crime may arise (Leff, Protess, & Brooks, 1986; O'Keefe, 1985). People may feel as fearful of the media world of crime as the real world, and lock their windows and stay home. If the news media cover stories about rape, then the public may begin to think about law and order, a long-standing issue in American political life (but, also see Protess, Leff, Brooks, & Gordon, 1985). If the press spotlights drug arrests and drug deaths, then this may stimulate both the public and officials to take action.

Yet the spotlight often moves swiftly, and as one political scientist discovered, legislators do not always regard as important the same issues as the press does (Gormley, 1975). The public may come to regard as important an issue in which leaders take little interest; the reverse may also happen (Gaziano, 1985). If the press spotlights issues, it may stimulate action, but there is also the possibility that nothing may happen. There are limitations to the agenda-setting role of the press.

The news media are hard pressed to cover issues in a fast-changing world. Lippmann (1922) was pessimistic that news fragments about events would add up to a coherent whole.

> everywhere it is assumed that the press should do spontaneously for us what primitive democracy imagined each of us could do spontaneously for himself, that every day and twice a day it will present us with a true picture of all the outer world in which we are interested. (p. 320)

The relationship between what the news media actually carry and what the public actually learns is extremely important. Thomas Jefferson said that if a hard choice had to be made between a government without newspapers and newspapers without a government, he would choose newspapers (Emery & Emery, 1988). We have faith that citizens learn enough about public issues to make intelligent choices on issues. There is an implied hope in agenda setting, that the press spotlight on events will linger long enough to illuminate issues for voters and leaders, and that leaders will take "proper" action.

Cook and her colleagues (Cook et al., 1983) summarized this hope in terms of investigative reporting.

> The classic "hypodermic" model of muckraking journalism would suggest that (1) journalists work on an investigation surrounded by as much secrecy as they can muster, (2) the investigative report then appears in print or is aired on television, (3) the public is aroused by the publication of the expose and (4) pressures elected officials or relevant agency personnel to correct the problem disclosed, and (5) these decision makers respond to the public and work to change the relevant policies. (p. 30)

But, these authors add, few would make the claim that the media-policy change linkage really works in any such orderly, linear way.

The ideal is based on both the public and leaders being energized by the news–and taking action. There also is the assumption that the news media will emphasize "good" issues–like the need to confront illicit drug use. Yet the news media must address many problems. And there is little time and few resources for investigative reporting.

SETTING THE AGENDA

Most journalists pick their stories from the cafeteria assortment of daily events, including the "budget" of suggested stories coming off the wire (McCombs & Shaw, 1976). We know that journalists are often influenced by each other, especially when trying to determine just what the news lead should be in an ambiguous situation (Crouse, 1972). What is news? That requires a decision and, because journalists read and view each other a great deal, there is also a consensus process at work. It takes a courageous journalist to be different, although some courageously are different and win Pulitzer prizes being so.

Significant information about how the press agenda is set by the stories appearing in two journalistic leaders, *The New York Times* and *The Washington Post*, is found in chapters 5 and 6. These detailed examinations show

how story ideas in general as well as specific information about drugs diffused from these two newspapers to other newspapers and the television networks. Understanding this process of interpress agenda setting is important both to communication scholars and to policymakers. It is important theoretically for our understanding of agenda building and how ideas and information are disseminated. There are practical implications for policymakers concerned with arousing public concern over drugs and with maintaining public support for government programs designed to combat the problem. Will the news and interpretative stories we read and view add up to a continuing social concern about drugs, and will the issue capture the attention of the public and government officials long enough for the society to take some kind of sensible action?

THE PROCESS OF AGENDA SETTING

There are many intervening variables between press coverage and action—some located in the press, some in the audience—to prevent a fully isomorphic match between press attention, public interest, and "official" response. Public issues are not all equal. Some issues, such as unemployment, can be obtrusive in our lives. These close-to-home issues can be so close, in fact, that they become part of the public agenda regardless of press attention, and may remain long after the news media spotlight has shifted to other issues on the public stage. Such issues are important whether the press deals with them or not (Weaver, Graber, McCombs, & Eyal, 1981). If there are several such obtrusive issues, then "new"—unobtrusive—issues may have to compete for the limited remaining spaces in the public agenda. The "mind" of the collective audience, both general public and leaders, is never free of existing issue concerns.

And of course readers and viewers vary in the amount of time spent with different types of mass media, in their level of political interest, in their sense of civic duty to keep up with the news, and in many other ways.

As members of the audience differ so do the mass media. Television and newspapers give issues immediate, but generally passing, attention. Some stories get headline treatment, some are on the back pages. Some are the lead on television; some are at the end. All these placement decisions can be reflected in readers' and viewers' assessments of issue importance. Political scientists Angus Campbell and Philip Converse have argued that national issues have gradually pushed out local ones as the mass media expanded to take so much of our attention in the 20th century, a finding with disturbing implications (Campbell & Converse, 1972). If issues disappear from the press, they can sometimes disappear from our attention. In November 1985, the government of South Africa banned television and print reporters from certain areas of racial turmoil in that country. By 1988, South Africa's apartheid seldom generated much student or activist attention and few presidential candidates in the primaries mentioned the issue. The issue has "disappeared"; apartheid has not.

OPTIMAL CONDITIONS FOR SETTING THE AGENDA

Issues can arise without media attention (Sohn, 1978), and they can linger as a residue after press attention shifts (Weaver et al., 1981). If an issue catches public attention, it may also catch the attention of leaders who can act, if leaders have the opportunity and political will. It is possible that mere attention to an issue can on occasion cause people to take action on their own. Scholar James Beniger (1978) found evidence that press attention to illicit drugs was related to a decline in drug use under some conditions.

Press attention does not always lead to action by readers, viewers, or leaders. Usually more is needed, the force of some kind of group or organization to push the agenda. America is full of organizations with special agendas—for example, on gun control, foreign policy, economic policy, women's issues, the environment. These groups have agendas that compete with or supplement press issues. But, together the combination can be powerful.

CONCLUSION

There are many "ifs" in the agenda-setting process. The press may move an issue on the public agenda if the press emphasizes it long enough, if the reading and viewing public is exposed to and interested in the issue, and if the public has room for the issue to penetrate its limited space for public issues. These "ifs" seem to hold across issues from world to national and local levels and to hold across both traditional political topics and at least some "nonpolitical" topics, such as drugs. For the nation to take personal or official action on its drug problem, both the press and public must participate. In a sense the press can set the agenda—when all "ifs" are met—but it cannot build a national agenda without a lot of public help.

It is not the job of the news media to create social policy. In our republic, that is the job of government and other leaders, supported by an informed public. To deal with illicit drugs, there are many private organizations that must be involved and there are many private organizations that can act. Many have. So has the press, especially recently. Through its agenda-setting role the press helps guide public and official thinking. But the press cannot tell us what to think and cannot act for us.

> The press is no substitute for institutions. It is like the beam of a searchlight that moves restlessly about, bringing one episode and then another out of darkness into vision. Men cannot do the work of the world by this light alone. They cannot govern society by episodes, incidents, and eruptions. It is only when they work by a steady light of their own, that the press, when it is turned upon them, reveals a situation intelligible enough for a popular decision. (Lippman, 1922, p. 364)

The agenda-setting role of the press is one of civic mobilization. The press helps focus our attention on the key problems of the days. It sets the agenda for public action. In a democratic society the press plays an indispensable role in helping achieve a working consensus of how public support and the resources of government and the private sector will be allocated to the concerns of the moment.

In the research presented here, we have learned a great deal about both press and public agendas in regard to drugs. Most importantly, we have gained additional insights into the dynamics of agenda building. There is excellent guidance here for those leaders and interest groups who wish to maintain public and governmental attention on drugs. There is an opportunity to be seized, but only a thoughtful policy extending beyond publicity of the moment will ameliorate the drug problem. The press and public agendas can be shaped by transitory events. But if the drug problem is to be reduced, neither the press nor public must be diverted by news events at the periphery of the issue. Using the knowledge presented here, a thoughtful leadership – in the press, government, and public – must frame the drug issue for the national agenda in such a way that ameliorating actions are possible.

REFERENCES

Beniger, J. R. (1978). Media content as social indicators. The Greenfield index of agenda-setting. *Communication Research, 5,* 437–453.

Campbell, A., & Converse, P. (Eds.). (1972). *The human meaning of social change.* New York: Russell Sage.

Cohen, B. (1963). *The press and foreign policy.* Princeton, NJ: Princeton University Press.

Cook. F.L., Tyler, T.R., Goetz, E.G., Gordon, M.T., Protess, D., Leff, D. R., & Molotch, H.R. (1972). Media and agenda-setting. Effects on the public, interest group leaders, policy makers, and policy. *Public Opinion Quarterly, 47,* 16–35.

Crouse, T. (1972). *The boys on the bus.* New York: Ballentine Books.

Emery, M., & Emery, E. (1988). *The press and America: An interpretative history of the mass media.* Englewood Cliffs, NJ: Prentice-Hall.

Gaziano, C. (1985). Neighborhood newspapers and neighborhood leaders: Influences on agenda setting and definitions of issues. *Communication Research, 12,* 568–594.

Gormley, W.T., Jr. (1975). Newspaper agendas and political elites. *Journalism Quarterly, 52,* 304–308.

Leff, D. R., Protess, D.L., & Brooks, S.C. (1986). Crusading journalism. Changing public attitudes and policy-making agendas. *Public Opinion Quarterly, 50,* 300–315.

Lippmann, W. (1922). *Public opinion.* New York: Macmillan.

McCombs, M.E., & Shaw, D.L. (1972). The agenda-setting function of mass media. *Public Opinion Quarterly, 36,* 176–187.

McCombs, M.E., & Shaw, D.L. (1976). Structuring the unseen environment. *Journal of Communication, 26,* 18–22.

Miller, G.A. (1956). The magic number seven, plus or minus two: Some limits on our capacity for processing information. *Psychological Review, 63,* 81–97.

O'Keefe, G.J. (1985). "Taking a bite out of crime": The impact of a public information campaign. *Communication Research, 12,* 147–178.

Protess, D.L., Leff, D.R., Brooks, S., & Gordon, M.T. (1985). Uncovering rape: The watchdog press and the limits of agenda setting. *Public Opinion Quarterly, 49,* 19–37.

Sohn, A.B. (1978). A longitudinal analysis of local non-political agenda-setting effects. *Journalism Quarterly, 55,* 325–333.

U.S. News & World Report, People who didn't say no. (1988, March 21) p. 73.

Weaver, D.H., Graber, D.A., McCombs, M.E., & Eyal, C.H. (1981). *Media agenda-setting in a presidential election: Issues, images, and interest.* New York: Praeger.

Author Index